A Pho

SEA FISHES

OF AUSTRALIA

Rudie H. Kuiter

First published in 1997 by
New Holland Publishers Pty Ltd
Sydney • London • Cape Town • Singapore

3/2 Aquatic Drive
Frenchs Forest
NSW 2086
Australia

24 Nutford Place
London W1H 6DQ
United Kingdom

80 McKenzie Street
Cape Town 8001
South Africa

Edited by Robyn Flemming
Typeset by DiZign
Reproduction by DNL Resources Pty Ltd
Printed by Times Offset (M) Sdn Bhd

National Library of Australia
Cataloguing-in-Publication data

Kuiter, R.H.
A photographic guide to sea fishes of Australia.

Includes index.
ISBN 1 86436 220 0.

1. Marine fishes - Australia - Identification. 2. Marine
fishes - Australia - Pictorial works. I. Title.

597.0994

Front cover: Juvenile Scalyfin
Title page: Redcoat Squirrelfish
Back cover: Regal Angelfish
Spine: Lined Surgeonfish

Contents

Introduction   4

How to use this book   5

Classification   5

External features of fish   6

Key to symbols   8

Species accounts   10

Glossary   140

Further reading   141

Index   142

Introduction

Australia is an island continent with a coastline almost 37 000km in length. The southern end of the continent reaches into temperate seas, bordering the Antarctic region, and the northern end lies in tropical zones near the equator. In addition, it divides the Pacific and Indian oceans in the Southern Hemisphere, supporting one of the most diverse fish fauna in the world. The fauna are very different not only between north and south, but between east and west as well. Fluctuations in currents and water temperature play an important role in causing variations in fauna from one part of the coast to the next, and most changes in local fauna occur where the coastline changes direction. With current patterns generally fixed, many points of change are identified around Australia, abruptly dividing some coastal habitats.

The physical make-up of habitats varies greatly along the coast and includes rocky, sandy or weedy environments, long surf beaches, and quiet inlets with input from fresh water, seagrasses, mangroves, etc. Combinations are endless, and sometimes small pockets of unique habitats are home for specific fishes that live nowhere else. The estuarine or protected bay habitats with seagrass beds, which in themselves are enormously diverse, are particularly difficult to categorise. The actual seagrass species, the type of bottom, the presence of reef, distance to the open sea, run-off from the land, and the depth and clarity of the water are just some of the factors influencing the diversity of a particular site.

With regard to behaviour and habitats, fishes could be compared to birds: pelagic fishes showing parallels with migrating birds, and reef fishes showing parallels with bush birds. Weed or kelp and coral habitats vary as much as the bush habitats. In the same way that birds are found in only specific places in relation to the kinds of trees or flowers that grow there, fishes live in various habitats in relation to specific corals or weeds.

The origin of Australian fishes is mixed. Fauna came from different directions during the continent's drift north, taking many of the original southern species with it, and arrival in the Indo-Malay region brought an additional fauna to the northern parts. Most of the fishes found in the southern temperate zones, including the subtropical areas such as New South Wales and the Lord Howe Island region, are descendants from Gondwana times when Australia was part of the Antarctic region. Most of these fishes are local endemics. The northern fishes took over the area that warmed over time and this fauna now extends to northern New South Wales where fishes of northern and southern origin overlap in range. Many of the northern-origin fishes are widespread in the tropical Indo-Pacific. Interestingly, some of the fishes of southern and northern origin share the same genus, and thus have changed relatively little when compared to the millions of years that have passed since they evolved from a common ancestor. Australia's terrestrial fauna is famous for unique creatures such as the platypus, the kangaroo and the koala, but equally as unique underwater are the Leafy Seadragon and handfishes in Tasmania, just to name a few that have no close relatives elsewhere in the world.

Several thousand species occur in the waters around Australia's coasts. The 222 fishes included in this book are the common or most often observed species, and a few of those that are of interest to diving fish-watchers. Representatives of most groups are included, and usually the more obvious ones that are likely to be noticed underwater. For more comprehensive coverage, see the suggested further reading (page 141).

How to use this book

Photographs are the main tool for identifying a particular fish. Silhouettes showing the principal outline for each different group are grouped together in the front of the book for easy reference. The same silhouettes are shown on the top corner of the pages in the species account, and similar species are grouped together. As not all species could be included, those similar to the one illustrated are treated in the text. When many similar species are involved, the text is more general. Different stages or colour forms are either illustrated with an additional photograph or described in the species account.

Identifying fishes underwater is not easy, even with good knowledge of them. Most difficult is trying to find a fish in the book that was seen during a dive. It requires training to remember certain features to work with, such as shape, type or number and placement of fins, and even simple facts such as whether stripes run horizontally or vertically. It is important to make mental notes when looking at a particular fish to be identified later. Using colour can be unreliable, and one needs to know the filtering effect of the water, which changes colour with depth. The photographs in the book were all taken with a flash, thus showing the fish in full colour as it would appear at the surface. With depth, red is filtered out and simply turns to grey; this works as camouflage against open backgrounds. Comparing photographs or a fish in hand is relatively easy, but if there are many similar species in a particular group it may require an expert to put a specific name to them.

The common name given is that used in Australia, followed by the scientific name that is the most recent and based mainly on scientific works. Size is given as total length (TL) for most fishes. Only in the case of some rays is the width given instead, as often the tail is damaged and length unreliable. Descriptions refer to identifying features of the fish and the habitat where the particular species is likely to be seen.

Classification

All the fishes in this book belong to the Superclass PISCES – they have jaws and paired fins (except for degenerated fins in some species). Superclass PISCES is made up of two main groups: Class CHONDRICHTHYES: cartilaginous fishes including sharks, rays and ghostsharks; and Class OSTEICHTHYES: bony fishes including eels, scorpionfishes, pipefishes, perch-like fishes and pufferfishes.

The 350 sharks and almost 500 ray species belong in about 15 orders and all have representatives in Australian waters. There are many families but these are generally not numerous.

The bony fishes represent an enormous assembly of vertebrate animals, and with about 20 000 species worldwide, they are by far the largest and most diverse group. The Order PERCIFORMES is the largest with around 150 families, and includes most of the fishes we eat such as snapper, bream and whiting. Other groups with many reprentatives in Australian waters are the SCORPAENIFORMES, which include scorpionfishes, lionfishes and stonefishes, (all of which have venomous spines); SYNGNATHIFORMES, including seahorses, seadragons and pipefishes; and the TETRAODONTIFORMES, which include the pufferfishes, leatherjackets, triggerfishes and porcupinefishes.

Other groups are either of less significance to Australian waters or are only represented in very small numbers. The species included in this book are representative of most groups that are found in Australian waters.

External features of fish

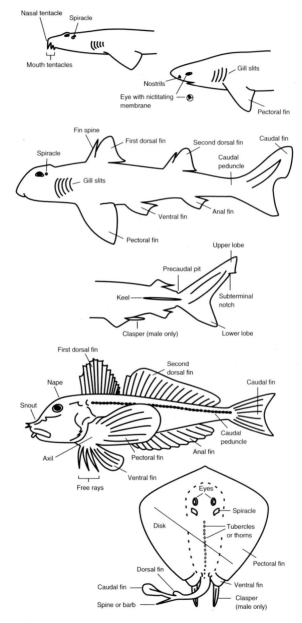

6

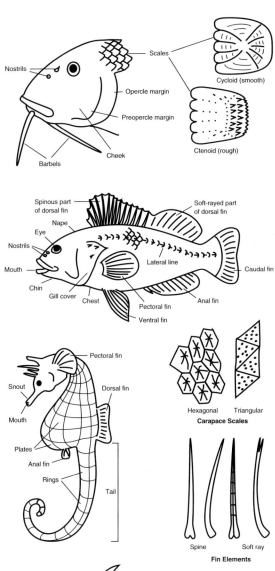

Scales

Cycloid (smooth)

Ctenoid (rough)

Nostrils

Opercle margin

Preopercle margin

Cheek

Barbels

Spinous part of dorsal fin

Soft-rayed part of dorsal fin

Nape

Eye

Nostrils

Mouth

Chin

Gill cover

Chest

Pectoral fin

Ventral fin

Anal fin

Lateral line

Caudal fin

Pectoral fin

Snout

Mouth

Plates

Anal fin

Rings

Dorsal fin

Tail

Hexagonal

Triangular

Carapace Scales

Spine

Soft ray

Fin Elements

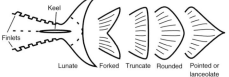

Keel

Finlets

Lunate

Forked

Truncate

Rounded

Pointed or lanceolate

Caudal Fin Shapes

Key to symbols

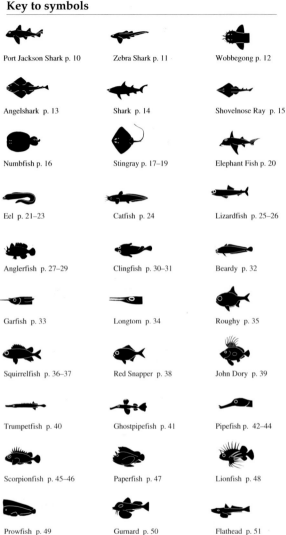

Port Jackson Shark p. 10

Zebra Shark p. 11

Wobbegong p. 12

Angelshark p. 13

Shark p. 14

Shovelnose Ray p. 15

Numbfish p. 16

Stingray p. 17–19

Elephant Fish p. 20

Eel p. 21–23

Catfish p. 24

Lizardfish p. 25–26

Anglerfish p. 27–29

Clingfish p. 30–31

Beardy p. 32

Garfish p. 33

Longtom p. 34

Roughy p. 35

Squirrelfish p. 36–37

Red Snapper p. 38

John Dory p. 39

Trumpetfish p. 40

Ghostpipefish p. 41

Pipefish p. 42–44

Scorpionfish p. 45–46

Paperfish p. 47

Lionfish p. 48

Prowfish p. 49

Gurnard p. 50

Flathead p. 51

Rockcod p. 52–55

Basslet p. 56–58

Blue Devil p. 59–61

Trumpeter p. 62

Bigeye p. 63

Cardinalfish p. 64–65

Trevally p. 66–68

Silverbelly p. 69

Bream p. 70–72

Sweetlips p. 73

Snapper p. 74–75

Fusilier p. 76

Goatfish p. 77

Bullseye p. 78

Sweep p. 79–80

Stripey p. 81–82

Butterflyfish p. 83–87

Bannerfish p. 88

Angelfish p. 89–91

Batfish p. 92

Boarfish p. 93

Old Wife p. 94

Morwong p. 95

Hawkfish p. 96–97

Damsel p. 98–102

Wrasse p. 103–110

Weedwhiting p. 111

Parrotfish p. 112–113

Grubfish p. 114

Blenny p. 115–117

Weedfish p. 118

Dragonet p. 119

Goby p. 120–122

Surgeonfish p. 123

Moorish Idol p. 124

Rabbitfish p. 125

Flounder p. 126–127

Triggerfish 128–129

Leatherjacket p. 130–132

Cowfish p. 133–134

Pufferfish p. 135–139

Port Jackson Shark *Heterodontus portusjacksoni* TL 1–1.6m

Adult

This shark is easily recognised by its shape and colour. It has a blunt head and a crest above each eye, most obvious in juveniles, and two large dorsal fins, each headed by a venomous spine. Port Jackson Sharks are non-aggressive and are usually found resting on substrate amongst rocks or under large ledges. They congregate in spring to mate, and the female produces spiral flanged egg cases in each of which a single young develops. Most egg cases are wedged between rocks but occasionally are found away from reefs. After about eight to ten months a 15 to 20cm long young wriggles free, and empty egg cases may wash up on certain bay-beaches in great numbers. Diet comprises various benthic invertebrates. The Port Jackson Shark belongs to a small family, the Horn Sharks, also known as Bullhead Sharks. The **Crested Horn Shark** (*H. galeatus*) has particularly high crests above the eyes but is a less common species and mainly restricted to New South Wales waters. The third Australian species, the **Zebra Horn Shark** (*H. zebra*) with a distinct banded pattern, is least known and is usually restricted to deep tropical waters.

Juvenile

Zebra Shark *Stegostoma fasciatum* TL 2.4–3.5m

Adult

Juveniles have strong zebra-like black-and-white banding, hence the common name. With growth, the banding gradually changes to the spotted adult pattern for which it is called the Leopard Shark. Adults develop very long tails, almost as long as the rest of the body. Usually seen singly but congregates in large numbers in some areas to mate. A non-aggressive shark, often found resting on sandy substrate during the day and behaviour is mostly nocturnal. Egg cases are golden-brown when laid and darken to near black with age. They have longitudinal striations, measuring about 18cm in length and width half of that. The young hatch when almost 20cm long. Diet comprises mostly benthic invertebrates and occasionally fishes. Single species in a family that is widespread in the tropical Indo-Pacific, and is closely related to wobbegongs.

Juvenile in aquarium

Spotted Wobbegong *Orectolobus maculatus* TL 3m

Adult

Wobbegongs grow large, and these sluggish looking sharks can be potentially dangerous when provoked. Of the six Australian wobbegongs, two are commonly encountered in coastal waters in the southern mainland states: the Spotted Wobbegong and the **Ornate** or **Banded Wobbegong** (*O. ornatus*), differing only slightly in colour by having bluish grey spotting and number of skinflaps around the mouth. The **Tasselled Wobbegong** (*Eucrossorhinus dasypogon*) is moderately common on coastal tropical reefs and is distinctive in its grey mottle colouration, with a greatly flattened body and a head with numerous tassels around its margin. The other species are rarely seen. The Spotted Wobbegong lives in various habitats from shallow estuaries to continental shelf. Eggs hatch inside the female, and young are born when about 20cm long. Litter sizes can be large, numbering up to 37. They sleep during the day on rocky ledges, in caves, or on sand among rubble and weeds, and hunt various benthic animals at night, preying on crustaceans, cephalopods and fishes.

Juvenile

Angelshark *Squatina australis* TL 1.5m

Adult

Also known as the Australian Angelshark or Monkfish, these fishes typically bury themselves in clean sand near reefs or seagrass beds, where they lie in ambush for squid, octopus or fish. They are perfectly shaped for the purpose: with their greatly flattened bodies, the body outline is barely visible when buried, and the eyes and open nostrils are usually only just visible. In addition, they have excellent camouflage: the body colour above matches the colour of the sand of the area, whilst underneath they are almost white. Angelsharks give birth to about ten young per litter, about 30cm in length. They are not aggressive but could bite if provoked or handled. There are four known Australian species, but most live in depths exceeding 100m and only one species is commonly encountered in the shallows.

Juvenile

Blacktip Reef Shark *Carcharhinus melanopterus* TL 1–1.4m

This fast small shark is not considered dangerous but could bite waders on the leg by mistake. It is easily recognised by the distinctive black fin-tips, especially on the dorsal fin and tail. Blacktip Reef Sharks usually measure about 50cm at birth, and juveniles form small schools. Large adults are often solitary, venturing into deep water and usually swimming low over sand. This is a very common tropical species in shallow depths, often hunting other fishes in subtidal zones, and is one of the species most noted by snorkellers.

Whitetip Reef Shark *Triaenodon obesus* TL 1.7–2.1m

This is a harmless species that feeds on small fish and invertebrates from the substrate. There are several similar 'white-tipped' sharks, referring to the white tips on the fins, but this species is the most slender and is associated with reefs. Generally shy, but in some areas where the sharks are used to divers they can be approached at close range. The young are about 50 to 60cm at birth. Whitetip Reef Sharks commonly occur in reef lagoons and along the base of deep walls and are usually seen swimming along reef walls or resting on sand patches below, sometimes forming loose groups.

Western Shovelnose Ray *Aptychotrema vincentiana* TL 80cm

Shovelnose rays have greatly flattened bodies and a long pointed snout. They are benthic fishes which partly bury themselves in or lay on the sand-substrate and match the surrounding colours. The different species are distinguished by less obvious features of the mouth, eyes, nostrils, length of snout and sometimes by colour pattern. The Western Shovelnose Ray is one of the best known Australian species. It feeds primarily on crabs and prawns and has small litters, two to eight embryos per egg capsule that hatch inside the female. It is mainly coastal, entering estuaries.

Eastern Fiddler Ray *Trygonorrhina fasciata* TL 1.2m

Fiddler rays are closely related to the shovelnose rays and differ primarily in having a broadly rounded snout. The Eastern Fiddler Ray can be distinguished from its southern cousin (*Trygonorrhina guaneria*) by the small triangle on the back, just behind the eyes. Fiddler rays congregate in the summer months to mate and are sometimes found crowding caves. Litters are small, and there are several young per egg capsule which hatch inside the female. Fiddler rays live in coastal waters, often on reefs and near seagrass beds, and feed on soft-shelled invertebrates.

Numbfish *Hypnos monopterygium* TL 40–60cm

The Numbfish is one of the electric rays and can give a powerful shock underwater, as well as above. Its colour is highly variable, from light brown to almost black, usually in relation to the habitat. Numbfishes are predators, taking surprisingly large fish, and are most active at night. Females gives birth to small young, just 10cm long. Numbfishes commonly occur on soft substrates, including mud and fine sand, where they bury themselves with their open nostrils just visible. They are found in shallow estuaries to deep offshore waters, reported to depths of over 200m. Only about four species are known from Australian waters. The only other species entering shallow depths is the **Tasmanian Numbfish** (*Narcine tasmaniensis*), but it is rarely seen in mainland waters.

Melbourne Skate *Raja whitleyi* TL 1.7m

 Skates lack the venomous spine found on the tail of many rays, but they do have thorny spines that could inflict wounds if not handled with care. Modern skates bear little resemblance to their shark-like ancestors with their greatly flattened and broad disc. The snout is usually pointed and extended in some species. Colour can change from light grey or brown to almost black, according to habitat. Skates are live bearers and feed mainly on small bottom-dwelling invertebrates and fishes. There are about 35 skates in Australian waters, but few enter shallow depths. The Melbourne Skate, sometimes called Whitley's Skate, enters shallow estuaries and can be seen in depths of a few metres. It is known to depths of 170m and is the largest Australian species, reaching a maximum weight of at least 50kg. The **Thornyback Skate** (*R. lemprieri*) is another species which enters shallow depths but only commonly in Tasmanian waters. The Thornyback Skate usually has a dark snout and sometimes the whole skate is dark grey.

Banded Stingaree *Urolophus cruciatus* TL 50cm

Stingarees are similar to stingrays, but their tail is not whip-like and usually has small fins at the tip and one or two venomous spines which can inflict extremely painful wounds. The distinctive Banded Stingaree, also known as the Cross-back Stingaree, has a lined or spotted dark pattern on the back. It gives birth to small litters of two to four young and feeds on a variety of bottom-dwelling creatures. It occurs commonly in shallow Tasmanian waters but usually moderately deep in coastal waters of the mainland, where occasionally it enters estuaries with seagrass beds.

Common Stingaree *Trygonoptera testacea* TL 45cm

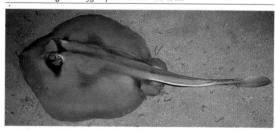

This well-camouflaged species is usually plain greyish brown in colouration over the top, matching the sand or mud, and often with dark shading below the eyes. Most stingarees prefer deep water and are active at night, hunting mainly crustaceans and small fishes, and bury themselves in sand or mud near reefs during the day. They are live bearers, giving birth to two to four young. The Common Stingaree is probably the most observed stingaree in New South Wales where it inhabits shallow bays and enters harbours or sandy estuaries. Several similar species are found along the southern half of Australia.

Blue-spotted Fantail Ray *Taeniura lymna* TL 70cm, width to 30cm

A small ray with bright blue spots that is often noticed by snorkellers in lagoons and on coral reefs. It often hides under coral plates and is active on dusk or at night. In some areas it feeds during the day on shallow flats when the tide is high. Litters are small, giving birth to few young. It feeds on shelled invertebrates which are exposed from the sand by blowing a jet of water from the mouth that is taken in through the large holes situated behind the eyes. Ranges to a depth of about 20m. Widespread in the tropical Indo-Pacific.

White-spotted Eagle Ray *Aetobatus narinari* Width to 3m

These distinctive rays are among the most graceful in tropical waters. They are fast swimmers, often forming large schools swimming well above the bottom or near the surface, and are sometimes seen jumping high into the air. They prefer open water and descend to the bottom to feed, mainly over extensive sand-flats between the shore and reefs in the afternoon. They expose prey by blowing away sand, feeding on invertebrates such as worms, shrimps, or octopus and squid or cuttlefish. In turn they are preyed upon by the large pelagic sharks. Litters produce up to about six young. Common throughout the tropical Indo-Pacific.

19

Elephant Fish *Callorhinchus milii* TL 1.2m

Adult (female)

A prehistoric-looking fish that belongs to a small group related to sharks and rays, but only has one gill-slit versus the usual five or six of sharks and rays. It looks shark-like, except for the head which features a rather unusual snout with an extension to probe the sand for prey. Elephant Fish are open-water swimmers and can cover great distances to migrate. They form schools and can swim very fast with their large pectoral fins like rays, seemingly flying along. During the summer months, great numbers of females enter large sandy estuaries to deposit their egg capsules in the upper reaches. Young hatch after about eight months in the following spring. (One capsule laid in the author's aquarium hatched after 221 days, producing a perfect miniature of the adult.) Elephant Fish feed primarily on molluscs dug out of the sand, taking other invertebrates that get in the way.

Hatchling

Banded Snake Eel *Myrichthys colubrinus* TL 97cm

The Banded Snake Eel moves about during the day in shallow lagoons and is often mistaken by snorkellers for a common sea snake. It has several colour variations. Usually it is white with black bands like rings around the body, but in some the dark bands are more like saddles over the back. There are many snake eel species, but most are secretive and bury themselves in the sand during the day and only come out at night to hunt. They feed primarily on small fishes or shrimps, and nothing is known about their reproduction. The Banded Snake Eel occurs throughout the tropical Indo-Pacific.

Ribbon Eel *Rhinomuraena quaesita* TL 1.2m

The bright blue body and yellow snout of this eel quickly catches the diver's attention. Juveniles to almost adult size are black with a yellow dorsal fin, and large females can be yellow all over. Their eyesight is poor; instead, they use their large flared-out nostril membranes

to scan their surroundings or scent small fishes. Ribbon Eels rarely leave their burrow and are most active on dusk. They occur on coastal to outer reef slopes from about 6 to 50m, in a mixed sand and reef habitat. They are widespread in the tropical Indo-Pacific, but are rarely seen in large numbers.

Honeycomb Moray *Gymnothorax favagineus* TL 2m

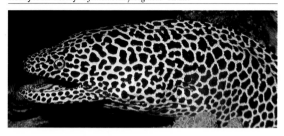

This distinctive moray eel is white with contrasting black spots, with the white interspaces forming a honeycomb pattern, but there are several similar species. The Honeycomb Moray is one of the largest morays, but reports of 3m length are doubtful. It is generally not aggressive but, like other morays in some areas during spawning time, it is unpredictable. Morays have been seen swimming towards the surface to release countless numbers of tiny eggs that float away in the currents. They feed on a variety of prey. The Honeycomb Moray commonly occurs on coastal reefs and is widespread in the tropical west Pacific.

Undulate Moray *Gymnothorax undulatus* TL 1m

An aggressive species that is identified by the combination of long snout, yellowish head, and a mosaic pattern created by large brown to black blotches. The long slender teeth can inflict a nasty wound. The Undulate Moray is common but rarely seen during the day. It almost exclusively hunts fishes at night which it seeks out by smell, checking small holes or crevices in the reef. It produces pelagic eggs, and occurs mainly on coastal reef slopes between 6 and 25m. It is one of the most observed eels when night-diving in the tropical Indo-Pacific where it is broadly distributed.

Green Moray *Gymnothorax prasinus* TL 1m

This eel is actually brown or yellow in colour, but when living in shallow depths its skin accumulates algae cells which gives it a green appearance. Green Morays are sometimes aggressive towards divers. Their teeth are needle-like and a bite can leave puncture marks. Large individuals can inflict a nasty wound. They feed primarily on crustaceans. Sometimes several individuals share a ledge and sit side by side, the mouth open in a seemingly threatening way. Well known to divers on the New South Wales coast, where it can be found in most habitats from rocky estuaries to offshore reefs.

White-eyed Moray *Siderea thyrsoidea* TL 65cm

This moray is easily recognised by the pearly-white eyes that stand out on the dark face. It has smaller and blunter teeth than other morays, feeding primarily on crus-taceans and worms, and is rather shy, retreating into its hole

when approached too closely. It is found in slightly silty habitats such as harbours, sheltered coastal bays and inner reefs, and on shipwrecks. It usually lives in depths of 10m or more. In New South Wales it lives mostly on coastal reefs in rocky ledges. It is a widespread species in the tropical west Pacific.

23

Striped Catfish *Plotosus lineatus* TL 35cm

Adults

The Striped Catfish, sometimes called the Coral Catfish, is often found in coastal waters where juveniles gather in tight balls over sand and mudflats. With growth, larger juveniles school more loosely and get together when threatened. Adults are in small groups or solitary but become secretive, living in the back of ledges during the day and coming out at night. Like other catfish, they have venomous spines heading the fins and should be handled with care. Repeated stings are potentially dangerous and can be fatal. Diet changes with growth: the young feed on detritus from mud surfaces, while adults prey on invertebrates or fishes. Striped Catfish live in coastal bays and enter estuaries. There are many catfishes in Australia but most are freshwater tropicals. This is one of the few marine species, and it occurs commonly and is widespread in the tropical Indo-Pacific, ranging into subtropical zones.

Juvenile

Sergeant Baker *Aulopus purpurissatus* TL 60cm

The male of this distinctively shaped species differs from juveniles and females by having greatly elongated filaments on the dorsal fin. A second dorsal fin made up of fatty tissue is known as an adipose fin. These fishes typically rest at high points on the bottom and strike at prey such as cephalopods but also take certain types of fishes coming within reach. They have rows of tiny needle-like teeth. They are mostly found on deeper coastal reefs with sponges and gorgonians and live to depths of 250m, but are sometimes found in shallower depths in harbours.

Painted Lizardfish *Trachinocephalus myops* TL 25cm

This species rarely stays above the sand surface, even for a few seconds. It buries itself until just the eyes are visible. Only when females are discovered by the male does some action take place above the sand, as it circles the female with erected fins. Painted Lizardfish lie in ambush for gobies or other small fish to come within striking reach. They live in sheltered sandy bays, often very shallow, and sometimes in the upper reaches of estuaries near the edge of seagrass beds. This single species in the genus is found in all tropical seas, sometimes ranging to subtropical zones.

Variegated Lizardfish *Synodus variegatus* TL 25cm

The Variegated Lizardfish is usually found on slightly elevated parts of reefs, from where it ambushes small fishes venturing too close. A blotched-banded colour pattern forms a series of irregular bars from just behind the head to the base of the tail. The colour is highly variable, and the blotches can change quickly from grey to near black or to red. There are a number of similar species, but most of these prefer to sit on sandy substrates and often bury themselves. The Variegated Lizardfish is most common on rock and coral reefs and is widespread throughout the tropical Indo-Pacific.

Blotched Saury *Saurida nebulosa* TL 16cm

Sauries are closely related to lizardfishes but differ in dentition and the ventral fin possesses a feeble spine. The jaws have several rows of numerous needle-like teeth to grasp prey. The Blotched Saury is one of the few species found on reefs, rather than sandflats, where it is well-camouflaged by the rubble bottom. It changes its colour and pattern to match the surroundings and is easily overlooked. Fishes swimming over the top are quickly grabbed and swallowed whole, and they can take surprisingly large prey. The Blotched Saury is widespread in the tropical Indo-Pacific.

Spotted Handfish *Brachionichthys hirsutus* TL 12cm

This was the first marine fish listed as endangered in Australia. The species was once common in the Derwent River estuary, Tasmania, and only a few populations remain. It is under threat from an introduced seastar that has no enemies and eats the eggs of handfishes which are laid on the bottom. Handfishes crawl along the bottom on their hand-like fins and only swim when disturbed. They feed primarily on worms. They are closely related to anglerfishes and are only found in southern Australian waters. Most species are endemic to Tasmanian waters, occurring in small localised populations.

Sargassum Anglerfish *Histrio histrio* TL 15cm

Finding this master of camouflage takes a keen eye, but giving a piece of floating weed a pull to see what is left behind gives results. The bulky body and weed-like colouration easily identifies this species. They feed on fishes or shrimps that seek protection in the weeds

from open-water predators, attracting them by wriggling a worm-like bait above the mouth. They produce numerous tiny eggs in a floating mucus mass amongst the weeds. The open-water surface habitat is also the reason for the species' wide distribution in all tropical seas except the east Pacific.

27

Tasselled Anglerfish *Rhycherus filamentosus* TL 23cm

When sitting on a rock surface, this fish is difficult to distinguish from algae. A temperate species, it is only known from Australia and, unlike tropical anglerfishes with floating egg rafts, it has demersal eggs. A large brood of about 5000 eggs, each about 5mm in diameter, is laid in a

rock crevice and guarded by the female. Young hatch after about 30 days and sink, crawling to the nearest crevice in the reef or under a rock. Adults congregate in early summer to breed. A worm-like bait attracts certain reef fishes for food. Inhabits shallow rocky reefs with algae and sponge growth.

Smooth Anglerfish *Phyllophryne scortea* TL 10cm

The most variable species of anglerfish on the south coast, the Smooth Anglerfish comes in a great range or combination of colours from bright yellow, orange or red to white and black, with saddle-like markings. It has a smooth skin on most of the body and short skinflaps around the mouth. Its bait unfolds into a replica of an amphipod to attract small sand-gobies (*Nesogobius* spp.). This species is restricted to Australian waters and is particularly common in South Australia on sheltered reefs and below jetties, where it hides under pieces of bryozoa or sponges lying on the bottom.

Striped Anglerfish *Antennarius striatus* TL 20cm

Striped Anglerfish are highly variable in colour, and sometimes the striped pattern is absent. The colour and stripes change to match the surroundings. Usually these fishes sit motionless on the bottom like a sponge, often next to a real one and matching its colour perfectly. A thick pinkish white worm-like bait is wriggled quickly to attract prey which includes a great variety of reef fishes. In Sydney Harbour they have been seen on several occasions to take seahorses. They can accommodate very large prey with an expandable stomach. The species is widespread in the tropical Indo-Pacific.

Clown Anglerfish *Antennarius maculatus* TL 10cm

Juveniles look like a brightly coloured nudibranch sitting on a dull background. There are some geographical variations: on the Great Barrier Reef the body is white with red markings and the fins have orange edges; and in many places they have a pale to bright yellow body. Adults are similar to juveniles and often as colourful as the young but develop wart-like swellings over the body. The bait resembles a small fish. Clown Anglerfish live in shallow protected coastal bays where they are usually on vertical rock faces that have short filamentous algal growth. The species is widespread in the tropical Indo-Pacific.

Long-snout Clingfish *Diademichthys lineatus* TL 50mm

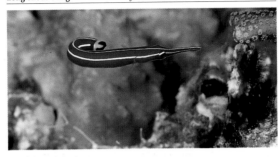

A small but interesting fish in appearance and behaviour. The slender body and very long snout when adult readily identifies this species. It swims by flicking its tail sideways and is usually seen in the vicinity of sea-urchins whose long spines provide protection for juveniles. Its eye is masked by the dark body stripes, and a spot in the tail could be mistaken for an eye, confusing predators by appearing back-to-front. There are several similar-looking striped clingfishes in the tropical seas, but most of these are secretive and lack the long snout. A common species on coral reefs.

Tasmanian Clingfish *Aspasmogaster tasmaniensis* TL 80mm

This species is usually strongly banded, especially over the head, but the general colouration is variable from pink to dark brown with dusky bands. The eye is often masked by a black stripe. Tasmanian Clingfish typically hide under small rocks in shallow, protected bays

and are often found by divers turning over rocks under jetties. Occasionally they can be found in rockpools, where they feed on small crustaceans such as mysids. There are several other species in this genus but the others are more secretive and have less distinctive colouration. This species is particularly common in the Bass Strait region.

Western Cleaner Clingfish *Cochleoceps bicolor* TL 70mm

This colourful clingfish, with orange or red spots and pale blue lines across, sometimes changes colour quickly and the back half is often darker than the front half. Unlike other clingfishes, it sits openly on sponges or ascidians where it is visited by reef fishes to be cleaned of parasites. In southern Western Australia it is not uncommon to see more than half a dozen individuals involved in cleaning large fishes. Eggs are laid on the base of the host or on nearby kelp where they are guarded by one or both parents. A common species on sponge reefs.

Shore Eel *Alabes dorsalis* TL 12cm

Shore Eels are a kind of clingfish without a suckerfin and have adapted to crawling on the bottom. They lack pectoral fins, and fin-rays are only present in the tail end. Their colour can vary from brown to orange or green, with or without spots or eye-like markings along the body. Males make a nest in narrow crevices and display to the female to entice her to lay eggs. The male guards the eggs until the tiny hatchlings emerge. Diet comprises small invertebrates. Shore Eels are found in rockpools and on shallow reefs in protected bays. They are common in Victoria.

Largetooth Beardy *Lotella rhacina* TL 40–66cm

Beardies are named after the chin-barbel that is a prominent feature beneath the mouth. The white margin along the fins is very distinctive, and body colour varies from dusky grey to reddish brown. There are several species – known as deepsea cods, rock cods, bearded rock cods or red cods – most of which live in deep water. They prey on cephalopods and small fish. The Largetooth Beardy lives in relatively shallow depths and is not as secretive as most. It lives on rocky reefs and has a preference for large caves and overhangs where it swims quite openly below, often in the front. This species is common in New South Wales, usually in depths of 10m or more, and is often found in pairs.

Grey – coastal variety

Southern Garfish *Hyporhamphus melanochir* TL 45cm

 Garfishes have an extended, beak-like lower jaw and are unlikely to be confused with other species. They school over seagrass beds where they spawn and drop their eggs. They are primarily surface fishes, swimming close to shore and in coastal bays. A few species have adapted to fresh water, and some live only in mangroves. Diet comprises algae, zooplankton, and insects taken on or close to the surface. They spawn above seagrasses and the eggs stick to the leaves. The Southern Garfish is closely related to the **Eastern Garfish** (*H. australis*), commonly found off New South Wales and southern Queensland, and their ranges overlap in southern New South Wales. Both species are popular with anglers in estuaries and they are often caught from jetties.

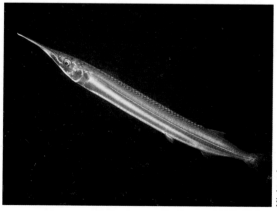

Night colour

33

Crocodile Longtom *Tylosurus crocodilus* TL 1.3m

Longtoms are surface fishes, very slender and silvery, and feature long, elongated jaws with numerous needle-like teeth. Often they swim alone, but sometimes form loose groups. They hunt small surface fishes inshore. In turn, they are hunted by the larger pelagic fishes and dolphins. They leap high into the air and continue over some distance with skips, seemingly 'walking' the surface on their tail. The Crocodile Longtom is a widespread species in the tropical Indo-Pacific and is the largest of all longtoms, reaching 5.2kg in weight. Some freshwater species only reach 10cm in length. There are 11 species known from Australian waters, but few range into southern waters as expatriates. Attracted by lights in boats, large longtoms have been known to cause fatal injuries to night fisherman with their spear-like beaks.

Roughy *Trachichthys australis* TL 18cm

Adult

Roughies produce a milky-looking poison from the skin when harassed. These fishes are easily recognised by their large bony head with obvious ridges and very large eyes. Small juveniles are different in colouration, black with a few large white blotches. Roughies live on rocky reefs in shallow depths in sheltered coastal bays and off-shore to over 40m in depth, and swim in the shade of overhangs in large ledges or caves during the day, moving out at night to hunt shrimps. They belong to a group known as sawbellies because of a series of enlarged scales along the belly called scutes. Some schooling species can produce loud clicking noises that enable individuals to keep in touch in the dark. The closely related **Orange Roughy** (*Hoplostethus atlanticus*) is commercially fished for in depths between 500 and 1000m. The Roughy is restricted to Australian waters and is sometimes called Pug-faced Roughy in New South Wales.

Juvenile

35

Redcoat Squirrelfish *Sargocentron rubrum* TL 27cm

This species forms large schools during the day, hovering near tall corals or caves, and moving out over open bottom at night to feed. It is identified by colour from other similar species. Squirrelfishes have strong spines in the fins and a prominent spine on the lower corner of the gill cover. The Redcoat Squirrelfish is mainly a coastal species, but is wide-ranging, with juveniles found as far south as Sydney in the summer months. This is one of the most common of several very similarly striped squirrelfishes. Most species are widespread in the tropical Indo-Pacific.

Giant Squirrelfish *Sargocentron spiniferum* TL 45cm

The largest of the squirrelfishes, this species is easily identified by the deep body shape and colour markings on the head. It varies in colour from grey to bright red, but the spinous or first dorsal fin is always red. It normally only raises this fin when alarmed. Depending on the area, adults swim alone or form schools during the day, usually hovering near large coral heads or caves, moving out to feed at night. Juveniles live in the back of ledges and are rarely seen. This species inhabits clear coastal reefs and deep outer reef lagoons and is widespread in the tropical Indo-Pacific.

Crimson Soldierfish *Myripristis murdjan* TL 25cm

This species is best identified by the strong white fin edges and slightly larger eye than in most similar species. Soldierfishes are difficult to identify underwater as there are about 20 similar species that are widespread in the tropical Indo-Pacific. The differences are often not obvious and limited to gill-raker or scale counts. They are nocturnal fishes that congregate in caves during the day, moving out at night and, depending on the species, feeding on the bottom on invertebrates or mid-water on plankton. The Crimson Soldierfish is a common coastal species, often entering shallow water.

Spotfin Squirrelfish *Neoniphon sammara* TL 24cm

This squirrelfish usually congregates in small groups around large coral pieces, especially those with shelf-like plates. The large spiny dorsal fin with the black blotch and white tips is a distinctive feature of the species. At night, individuals are solitary hunters, feeding on crustaceans, mainly shrimps. There are a few species in this genus, but they are much less common than the Spotfin Squirrelfish and are usually found in relatively deep water. This species occurs in clearwater lagoons and inner reefs and is widespread in the tropical Indo-Pacific.

Red Snapper *Centroberyx gerrardi* TL 46cm

Large adult

This is a member of a small global family of deepwater fishes which is not related to the common southern snapper or tropical snappers, and only superficially resembles them. It is best distinguished from the related nannygai species by the white edges on the fins and usually a white line centrally along the body. Also, it has large, bright-red eyes. Other members are known as alfonsinos, which are restricted to deep water in the northern and southern hemispheres, and the nannygais that are found mainly in Australian and New Zealand waters. Nannygais form great schools, but the Red Snapper is usually solitary and found in caves or amongst large boulders in much shallower water than the other species. However, it has been recorded to depths of 300m. The Red Snapper is common in the western part of its range.

Small adult

John Dory *Zeus faber* TL 66cm

This fish is easily recognised by the shape of its body, head and fins, all of which have distinctive features. It is deep-bodied, and on the middle of the sides it usually has a large dark blotch with a pale ring around it, forming a false eye. The head has a square shape when seen from the side with a large protrusible mouth, and the dorsal fin has long extended spines. This solitary hunter targets small fishes which are sucked in by the tube-like mouth when fully extended. Usually the John Dory occurs in deep waters, ranging most commonly between 60 and 400m, but in some areas it ventures into very shallow depths to pursue prey. It is one of the most widespread fishes, found in warm-temperate seas in both hemispheres of the Indian, Pacific and Atlantic oceans.

Close-up

39

Trumpetfish *Aulostomus chinensis* TL 60–90cm

The colour of this species is highly variable: juveniles are dull brownish grey with banded or striped patterns, and adults are sometimes bright yellow all over. It is easily recognised by its long body and large head. The snout is long and tubular with a small mouth at the tip which can open to take surprisingly large prey; primarily fishes that are targeted by adults in a cunning way by hiding or riding in the shadow of large and harmless fishes. Juveniles stay close to the bottom and are often with seafans. Trumpetfishes occur along slopes and walls from coastal to outer reefs. There are only two trumpetfishes, divided between the Pacific and Atlantic oceans. The Pacific species is widespread in tropical waters, and in Australia it ranges into subtropical zones when the larval stages are transported south by currents.

Ornate Ghostpipefish *Solenostomus paradoxus* TL 10cm

 These strange but beautiful little fishes are related to pipefishes and seahorses. The head looks the same and the body is similarly covered with bony plates, but they have more and much larger fins than pipefishes. Colour is highly variable and usually comprises several colours in a series of blotches or speckles with some large streaks or spots in the fins. Ghostpipefishes usually stay close to a suitable background such as seafans or featherstars, against which they have excellent camouflage, and float almost motionless with the head down. They feed mainly on tiny crustaceans that swim above the sand or on zooplankton drifting past. The female incubates her eggs between the large ventral fins that form a pouch by being held together and hooked on to small body spines. This species is widespread in the tropical Indo-Pacific and seasonally common in coastal bays where pelagic larvae drift in.

White's Seahorse *Hippocampus whitei* TL 20cm

There are several similar tropical species which are usually identified by the knob on top of the head, or crown. White's Seahorse has a distinctive crown with several knobby bits. Like most seahorses, it is highly variable in colour and matches its environment. It usually lives in pairs and produces young monthly during the breeding time. The male incubates the eggs and gives birth. Hatchlings settle on the substrate when they are born. Habitats range from shallow seagrass beds to moderate depths where they hang on to sponges. White's Seahorse is common in New South Wales, ranging north to Fraser Island in Queensland.

Short-head Seahorse *Hippocampus breviceps* TL 12cm

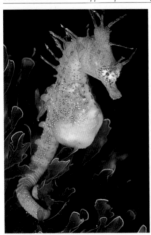

This small species is usually found in sargassum weeds growing on low rocky reefs with a lot of sand nearby or in small groups in shallow protected bays. The shallow water dwellers are usually a drab brown or grey, and often have long filaments over the back and on top of the head. Unlike tropical male seahorses that mainly change colour, the temperate species inflate their pouch to impress the female when courting. Hatchlings rise to the surface and grab on to floating weed, living a pelagic life for a few weeks. This species is common in the Bass Strait region.

Weedy Seadragon *Phyllopteryx taeniolatus* TL 45cm

Adult Weedy Seadragons are easily recognised by shape and colour, but colour varies with depth. Females become very deep-bodied with age. Males and juveniles are slender, and juveniles have much larger leafy bits on the spine. Males incubate about 250 eggs under the tail, each partly embedded into the skin. The young immediately swim and have to fend for themselves. Usually they have only one brood per season. Seadragons are unique to southern Australian waters. This is the most widespread of the two species and is commonly encountered along rocky shores in New South Wales and in Victorian and Tasmanian bays.

Leafy Seadragon *Phycodurus eques* TL 35cm

This spectacular Australian fish is a marvel of evolution. Adults are readily recognised by their shape and the large leafy appendages attached to the principal body spines. It lives in kelp and weed-dominated reefs and floats over the sand to hunt small crustaceans. Young feed almost exclusively on mysids. Their excellent camouflage enables them

to go about undetected by predator or prey. Even when floating over open sand they are easily missed, looking just like a piece of weed. Males carry eggs during November and December, migrating to sheltered parts of shallow reef. Common in coastal bays of South Australia and southern Western Australia.

Tiger Pipefish *Filicampus tigris* TL 30cm

Adult

This large and solid species is usually found lying on open sand or rubble patches in shallow protected bays. It is best identified by the series of white, evenly spaced spots along the lower side of the body. Adults have blue bars on the back. There are more than 100 species of pipefish living on reefs along Australia's coast and most are secretive or perfectly camouflaged. Identification underwater is very difficult, and even when collected many need to be identified by an expert. Most species live amongst weeds, but some tropical species swim in caves. Eggs are incubated by the male, usually protected by skin-flaps. The Tiger Pipefish is often noticed because of its large size and the fact that it is found out in the open. It is common in Sydney Harbour near the Heads.

Juvenile

Fortesque *Centropogon australis* TL 14cm

This is a kind of scorpionfish whose dorsal fin spines can inflict a painful sting. Colour can change quickly for camouflage purposes, but is light grey with almost black areas on the body. They sometimes congregate in large numbers, carpeting the bottom along reef margins on sand or rubble. Small juveniles are often in seagrass beds. Like most scorpionfishes, eggs are probably pelagic. Common in New South Wales estuaries. The **Northern Fortesque** (*C. marmoratus*) is similar but has a lower dorsal fin, and is more tropical and apparently restricted to coastal Queensland. The **Western Fortesque** (*C. latifrons*) is confined to the south-west coast.

Ruddy Gurnard Perch *Neosebastes scorpaenoides* TL 40cm

This large scorpionfish is often found on the sand adjacent to rocky reef or sponges, from shallow coastal bays to deep offshore. Most other species in the genus are restricted to depths of 100m or more. Gurnard perches are active at dusk and at night, feeding on a variety of invertebrates such as squid and shrimps, but also small fishes. The Ruddy Gurnard Perch changes shape with growth, and the proportionally large head is usually only developed in adults. It is very well camouflaged and more often noticed at night, showing its colours better in artificial light.

45

Red Rockcod *Scorpaena cardinalis* TL 40cm

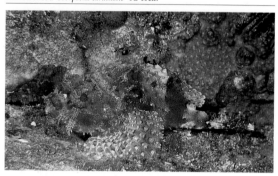

This large and robust species relies on its excellent camouflage to escape detection. The colour is highly variable, matching rocks and sponges or associated growth, changing to red in deep water. Often they have leafy skin bits growing over the body and large leafy tentacles above the eyes. The species is common on off-shore reefs with sponges and ranges to deep water, but enters rocky estuaries as well. They feed on cephalopods, fishes and shrimps. The similar **Western Rockcod** (*S. sumptuosa*) inhabits southern Western Australia and the **Southern Rockcod** (*S. papillosa*) Tasmania and the Bass Strait region along the mainland.

Pygmy Rockcod *Scorpaenodes scaber* TL 12cm

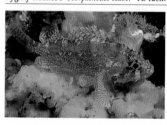

This is one of the most southerly species of a group of small tropical and very similar looking scorpionfishes. Colour varies from pink to red. They favour rock walls with crevices and caves, and sometimes small groups can be found hanging upside down on

the ceilings of large overhangs. During the day they stay in narrow crevices in the back of reefs, moving out over the rocks at night, feeding primarily on crustaceans. The Pygmy Rockcod is particularly common in New South Wales on rocky reefs and in harbours, as well as offshore in deep water.

Paperfish *Taenianotus triacanthus* TL 10cm

This small but interesting scorpionfish, with an extremely flat body compressed sideways into a tall leaf-like shape, is sometimes called the Leaf Scorpionfish. Colour varies drastically from almost white to yellow, green and even bright pink, often with dark and light spotting or scribbling. It perches itself with the large pectoral fins between corals or sponges and often sways sideways as if it were being pushed by the wash of a wave. Some individuals can be found in the exact same spot every day. Occasionally the Paperfish occurs in pairs. This species is widespread in the tropical Indo-Pacific, and is usually found on shallow and clear coastal reefs but has been recorded to a depth of 135m.

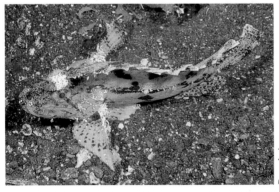

Dorsal view

Common Lionfish *Pterois volitans* TL 35cm

The dorsal spines of the lionfish, one of the best known scorpionfishes, are highly venomous and a sting produces instant excruciating pain. The Common Lionfish is variable in colour and some features, such as the leafy tentacles above the eyes that are usually large in juveniles, can be absent in some adult populations. The species is commonly encountered on tropical reefs in various habitats from shallow estuaries to deep offshore. Juveniles are carried beyond the normal breeding range by currents during their pelagic larval stage. The very similar **Russell's Lionfish** (*P. russelli*) is not well known in Australian waters.

Zebra Lionfish *Dendrochirus zebra* TL 20cm

This distinctively coloured lionfish has alternating broad and thin body banding and large webbing of the pectoral fins with the ray extending only slightly beyond the border of the fins. A smallish species, specimens 10cm long are often observed on reefs. Larger individuals seem to prefer to inhabit caves, and small groups are often

seen suspended from large overhangs. Small juveniles are often in small groups on isolated outcrops of algae-covered rocks on open bottom. Occur in harbours and coastal bays but are mainly found on protected inner reefs in shallow depths, often congregating in small groups, and down to at least 80m.

Warty Prowfish *Aetapcus maculatus* TL 22cm

 Looking like a piece of sponge, this fish is easily overlooked; usually, it is found by accident. It lives under rocks on reefs or in small caves and varies its colour according to the habitat. Prowfishes are unique temperate Australian fishes that are unusual in lacking ventral fins which are compensated for by having large pectoral fins. They rarely swim, and when made to, they push water out of the gill opening giving them jet-propulsion. Adult Warty Prowfishes have lumpy skin, but the young are smooth and at one stage were thought to be a different species. Diet comprises shrimps and mysids. There are only two more prowfish species: the **Whiskered Prowfish** (*Neopataecus waterhousii*), in which the tail fin is separate, mainly known from southern Western Australia but ranging to Victoria; and the **Red Indianfish** (*Pataecus fronto*), in which the dorsal fin is very tall above the snout, ranging along the southern mainland coast, except Victoria.

Eastern Spiny Gurnard *Lepidotrigla pleuracanthica* TL 16–20cm

 Gurnards have very large pectoral fins and several strong and separate rays in the front that are used to walk and dig in the bottom. The large webbed pectoral fins are used to startle predators by suddenly spreading them and showing the bright colouration, often featuring large eye-like spots, but the fins are also used to corner small prey against the reef. Gurnards feed on shrimps and small fish and hunt on sand adjacent to reefs or seagrass beds. Most gurnards live in deep water and are mainly known from trawls and line fishing, but two species of spiny gurnards are commonly found in shallow depths. The **Southern Spiny Gurnard** (*L. papilio*) lives along the south coast and Tasmania, and the Eastern Spiny Gurnard is only known from the east coast.

Sand Flathead *Platycephalus bassensis* TL 46cm

The Sand Flathead congregates in loose groups in estuaries and coastal bays. The tail has a distinctive colour pattern and, like many similar species, is diagnostic for the Sand Flathead. Flatheads are easily recognised by the greatly depressed head that usually bears bony ridges with a series of spines. The large spines protrude backwards from the gill plates. Eggs are pelagic. Diet includes small fishes and a variety of creatures such as shrimps or squid. Most species are found on sand, where they bury themselves with just the eyes exposed. A large number are tropical and small. The Australian temperate species grows large, the largest being the east coast **Dusky Flathead** (*P. fuscus*) which reaches over 1m in length. The latter species was observed in pairs for spawning.

Large adult

Eastern Wirrah *Acanthistius ocellatus* TL 45cm

Wirrahs are a kind of grouper or rockcod, closely related to seaperches. Eastern Wirrah, like the **Western Wirrah** (*A. serratus*), are deep-bodied and have a spotted body pattern. They like caves and rocky ledges, often swimming along the front. They are opportunistic feeders but most active at dusk when many fishes are looking to shelter in a safe place for the night. Young can be found in rockpools and shallow reefs in protected coastal bays. Adults live in various rocky habitats from silty bays to offshore, to depths of at least 100m. Unlike groupers, wirrah are poor eating.

Harlequin Fish *Othos dentex* TL 76cm

The Harlequin is an inquisitive, brightly coloured fish with dark spotting and large yellow patches along the lower sides of the body. It has a large head and the eyes are placed high. It is often perched on the bottom of caves or on ledges with cleaner clingfishes to depths of about

30m. Although it looks similar to the tropical coral trouts, this is a temperate species that is closely related to seaperches and restricted to Australian waters. A common species on oceanic reefs with kelp and sponges in South Australia and southern Western Australia. It ranges to Victoria but is less well known there.

Coral Rockcod *Cephalopholis miniata* TL 40cm

Adults are brightly coloured from orange to red, with numerous blue spots all over that are close-set on the tail. Small juveniles are plain orange. Sometimes adults form small groups that swim about openly or shelter under large plate and table corals, but juveniles are solitary and secretive. The Coral Rockcod is a regular visitor to shrimp cleaning stations where shrimps check the teeth for food remains, opening its mouth wide with the shrimp walking over the teeth. Mainly found on clear coastal to outer reefs, along walls and in rich coral growth lagoons. Widespread and widely observed species in the tropical Indo-Pacific.

Footballer Cod *Plectropomus laevis* TL 1m

Small juveniles are white with black saddles, and swim about openly on reefs, apparently mimicking poisonous pufferfishes. The juvenile's colouration often persists in large individuals, but the saddle-like banding becomes obscured by general darkening of the body and blue spotting all over. Large adults are usually adjacent to very deep water and are

sometimes seen in small groups hovering near large reef outcrops in current-prone areas. They are most active at dusk, feeding on cephalopods and fish. Other species in the genus are usually known as coral trouts. The Footballer Cod, sometimes called Tiger Trout, is a widespread tropical Indo-Pacific species.

Bar-cheek Coral Trout *Plectropomus maculatus* TL 75cm

Individuals inhabiting shallow water are pale red-brown, becoming a deeper red in deep water, with large blue spots over the body and head. In adults the spots elongate on the head into a series of large dashes. The very similar **Coral Trout** (*P. leopardus*) has smaller and more numerous spots. These fishes are popular with anglers, and apart from hard-fighting are considered as excellent to eat. Whilst the genus is broadly distributed, the species have a limited distribution in the tropical Indo-Pacific. The Bar-cheek Coral Trout is a common coastal reef species, often very shallow on algae-covered reefs.

Long-finned Cod *Epinephelus quoyanus* TL 35cm

This cod is a kind of grouper (also called rock-cods in Australia). The Long-finned Cod has rather large pectoral fins which it uses to balance on the bottom. There are several very similar species; usually they are identified by the size of the spots on the head or some saddle-like spots over the back. They feed on a variety of invertebrates and fishes. The Long-finned Cod likes silty reefs and is commonly seen along the fringes of coastal reefs resting on the sand against remote outcrops of rock or coral. Broadly distributed in the tropical Indo-Pacific.

Red-barred Rockcod *Epinephelus fasciatus* TL 35cm

This species has distinctive red to brown broad banding on the body and black-and-white tips on the dorsal fin. Lives in a variety of habitats from sheltered harbours to exposed and surge reefs amongst rocky boulders, often in a few metres depth and are locally common. Small juveniles, typical for the genus, are secretive in reefs, in small caves and crevices, or amongst small boulders. They feed on shrimps, cephalopods and fishes. This is one of the most common species on shallow reefs. Thought to be a broadly distributed species in the tropical Indo-Pacific, but there are several geographical variations that may represent sub-species.

Banded Seaperch *Hypoplectrodes nigroruber* TL 30cm

A common southern species with large eyes bulging forwards on the top of the head. Colour is variable from black to red bands and sometimes yellowish. Diet comprises small crustaceans and fishes. There are several banded species. Best known is the **Half-banded Seaperch** (*H. maccullochi*) which occurs abundantly on New South Wales

rocky coastal reefs. The **Black-banded Seaperch** (*H. annulatus*) also occurs on the east coast and lives in caves, usually hanging upside down on the ceiling. The Banded Seaperch is commonly observed in Western Australia. This small group of fishes is restricted to subtropical Australia and the southern Pacific.

Orange Basslet *Pseudanthias squamipinnis* TL 12cm

Orange Basslets congregate in current-prone areas in coastal waters and in some oceanic locations they cloud the water when feeding. The bright-orange females often swim in schools in shallow waters to feed on zooplankton. The purplish males are less numerous and are usually busy displaying to females or showing off to other males. Small juveniles are bright orange and are sometimes called goldfish. They swim close to the reef, sheltering in narrow crevices with sea-urchins for protection. This is a wide-ranging species in the tropical Indo-Pacific but expatriates well into subtropical zones. Several geographical variations are possibly separate species.

Red Basslet *Pseudanthias cooperi* TL 12cm

This dark-red fish looks blue or grey with natural light in deep water. Juveniles are best identified by the greenish red colour and the dark streak from below the eye over the cheek. Adults develop a vertical dark bar centrally on the side of the body. Males turn very pale when displaying to females. Adults prefer depths of 20m or more and swim in schools above coral plates or reefs, along the bottom of walls, or in channels where currents are common. Juveniles shelter on coastal and outer reefs in various depths. Broadly distributed in the tropical Indo-Pacific, and juveniles expatriate into subtropical zones.

Mirror Basslet *Pseudanthias pleurotaenia* TL 15cm

A spectacular and large basslet species. Males and females form their own groups. Males usually have a large square blotch on their sides that looks deep blue with natural light. Displaying males change colour quickly, the body often turning pink and the ventral fins deep red. They often feed away from reefs where they also display to each other, but display to females close to reefs. Females are bright orange and feed in open water on plankton. In Australia, found usually in depths of about 30m or more and along the bottom of deep outer reef walls. This species is widespread in the tropical Indo-Pacific.

Fairy Basslet *Pseudanthias dispar* TL 9cm

Fairy Basslets typically form large schools along the upper margin of outer reef walls with rich coral growth, and where currents carry plankton from lagoons behind the reefs. Males are easily recognised by the red dorsal fin and long extended filamentous spine in the ventral fin. Females are plain orange with a rather pointed snout. Males often

swim in their own groups away from reefs and display to females close to the bottom. They turn on the brightest colours when displaying to each other. Juveniles and females form their own schools of same-sized individuals, usually staying close to the bottom.

Barber Perch *Caesioperca rasor* TL 25cm

The Barber Perch is an Australian temperate species closely related to the tropical basslets, and like other temperate species it grows much larger than its tropical cousins. Adults form large schools on reefs in tidal channels and deep offshore reefs, feeding high above reefs in open water on zooplankton. Juveniles are solitary or form small groups that become more numerous with age. They are more secretive than adults and live closer to the bottom. Males become very colourful with iridescent blue spots and scribbles, and often have a black bar or spot centrally on their sides.

Yellow Emperor *Diploprion bifasciatum* TL 25cm

The Yellow Emperor is a kind of soapfish, one of a small group of fishes that have a toxin in the skin. The toxin foams up when mixed with water and looks milky when released underwater. It is a distinctive species in colour and shape. Adults are grey to pale yellow and occasionally have a

black body. Small juveniles in Australia are bright yellow with black over the eyes and over the middle of the body. They feed primarily on fishes and take surprisingly large prey. Yellow Emperors occur mainly on coastal, often silty reefs and sometimes congregate in small numbers on shipwrecks or under jetties.

Multicolour Dottyback *Ogilbyina novaehollandiae* TL 10cm

This colourful small fish can vary from green with pink to black, and the fins have thin iridescent blue edges. Most dottyback species are very territorial and especially aggressive towards both their own kind and closely related species that could be competition. Eggs are deposited in narrow crevices and guarded by the male or both sexes. Dottybacks feed primarily on small invertebrates but take almost anything that moves and is not too big for the mouth. It is locally common on protected inshore reefs, swimming close to the bottom through channels and crevices looking for small prey. Restricted to the central and southern Queensland reefs.

Two-tone Dottyback *Pseudochromis paccagnellae* TL 60mm

The bright yellow and deep pink colouration is distinctive. The pink looks blue at depths. A solitary species, but often several individuals are present, each with their own territory, at reef sections that suit them, especially around caves with rich invertebrate growth such as sponges and soft corals. Normally this fish lives along deep drop-offs where it swims close to the bottom of caves or through crevices. Occurs on clear coastal to outer reef slopes and walls. A single widespread species is recognised in the tropical west Pacific, but the Australian form has a slightly different colour pattern.

Eastern Hulafish *Trachinops taeniatus* TL 10cm

Hulafishes are unusually elongated compared to other members of the family. Most common are the **Noarlungae Hulafish** (*T. noarlungae*) from South Australia and Western Australia, the **Southern Hulafish** (*T. caudimaculatus*) from Victoria and Tasmania, and the Eastern Hulafish, the most colourful hulafish species. It is bright red, black, white and yellow, occasionally with a bright-yellow back. They form large schools on coastal reefs, feeding high above the bottom on zooplankton. Eggs are laid in reefs, and the male guards the eggs by wrapping its long body around the brood. The hatchlings are pelagic. Unique to southern Australian waters.

Southern Blue Devil *Paraplesiops meleagris* TL 33cm

This beautiful reef species is friendly and often approaches divers. Small juveniles have rounded fins and are a pale blue with mainly bright-blue spots on the head and a broad black edge on the tail fin. In adults the dorsal and anal fin develop long trailing corners, sometimes reaching as far as

the tail. Eggs are laid on rock surfaces of narrow channels and guarded by the male or both parents. Despite the large mouth they seem to prefer small invertebrates as prey. Juveniles live in the back of caves. This species is common on southern coastal reefs.

Eastern Blue Devil *Paraplesiops bleekeri* TL 40cm

Adult

Like its southern cousin, this fish is very popular with New South Wales divers. It is easily recognised by the broad body banding and bright yellow on the fins. Juveniles are secretive in the back of far-reaching crevices, but adults are often seen in the front of caves, in many areas unafraid of divers. However, most stay in the shade of overhangs or live in the darker caves. In Jervis Bay the Eastern Blue Devil can be found on shallow rocky reefs just a few metres deep, but in most areas it lives on coastal reefs in depths of 10m or more. This species is common on some coastal reefs, mainly south of Sydney.

Juvenile

West Australian Jewfish *Glaucosoma hebraicum* TL 1.2m

Large adults are an impressive fish and often approach divers. Juveniles have four or five dark stripes along the body, whilst adults are plain silvery and show a more-or-less distinct band over the eye. As there are no other similar species in the area, it is easily recognised by its shape and colour. Juveniles are solitary and can be found shallow on reefs in protected coastal bays. Adults often pair and usually live deep, using large reef outcrops on sand as home. The species is restricted to southern Western Australia, but a very similar fish occurs in the China seas and Japan.

Western Striped Trumpeter *Pelates octolineatus* TL 28cm

Trumpeters can produce loud noises with their swimbladder when caught on a line, giving them other names such as grunters. The Western Striped Trumpeter has about eight stripes. Trumpeters are primarily marine, living in coastal waters, but some enter fresh water or have adapted completely. Some of the closely related Australian freshwater grunter species reach a good size and are good eating. Marine species are mainly small and regarded as trash fish. Juveniles live secretively in seagrasses, and adults swim about openly near reefs in schools. This species is restricted to south-western coastal bays and estuaries.

Crescent-tail Bigeye *Priacanthus hamrur* TL 40cm

Several similar bigeyes are sometimes called glasseyes because of their very large clear eyes. The Crescent-tail Bigeye is best recognised by the large lunate-shaped tail that is usually rounded or with a straight posterior edge in other species. The colour varies with depth or the mood of the fish, from pale silvery grey to bright red, and sometimes it shows a dark banded pattern. At night they feed mid-water on zooplankton and, despite their large mouth, target small prey that are filtered from the water with their numerous gill-rakers. Eggs are pelagic, and larvae settle from when about 30mm long. They are nocturnal fishes, usually found in or close to caves, sometimes forming small groups in coastal areas but may school in some oceanic locations.

Banded pattern

63

Tiger Cardinalfish *Cheilodipterus macrodon* TL 22cm

Large individuals have clearly visible teeth. Juveniles have thick stripes, a large black spot on the tail-fin base, and yellow eyes and snout. Adults have numerous lines, and often some yellow remaining on the snout. Adults solitary but occasionally in pairs. Prefer still, shady habitats along reef walls with small caves or narrow crevices during the day. At night they venture out over open bottom or reef to hunt small prey. All cardinals are mouth brooders and the male Tiger Cardinalfish incubates the eggs. A common tropical species; only expatriates range to the southern areas.

Southern Orange-lined Cardinalfish *Apogon properuptus* TL 85mm

One of several similar and often confused species which is distinguished from the others by the broad orange stripes that are much thicker than the pale grey interspaces and the solid orange belly. Usually identified as the wide-ranging **Orange-lined Cardinalfish** (*A. cyanosoma*) which has thin orange lines. The Southern Orange-lined Cardinalfish forms small groups or pairs in 3 to 30m depth on clear coastal to outer reefs during the day. At night, it ventures away from reefs over the sand bottom, feeding on small shrimps. Ranges north from Australia to eastern New Guinea and from southern Indonesia to Java.

Sydney Cardinalfish *Apogon limenus* TL 14cm

A large striped species with a restricted range on the east coast. Several other similar species differ in the number or thickness of lines along the body and the spot on the tail-fin base. During the day, the Sydney Cardinalfish congregates in caves and below large overhangs of rock above sand in still bays and in deeper water offshore, not affected by swell. Swims over sand at night to hunt shrimps. Males incubate the eggs in their mouth. Common in the Sydney area, particularly in Sydney Harbour. The very similar **Western Striped Cardinalfish** (*A. victoriae*) is restricted to the west coast at a similar latitude.

Southern Gobbleguts *Vincentia conspersa* TL 14cm

Usually greyish brown, but sometimes reddish brown when in deep water, this nocturnal species swims or floats just above the bottom to detect swimming prey, and hides or swims in the back of large dark caves during the day. Like their tropical cousins, this cardinal is a mouth brooder and the male

incubates the eggs. It is the only large cardinalfish found in shallow waters of Tasmania and southern Victoria, where they are common on shallow to deep rocky reefs. The South Australian population is a more speckled variation, and almost identical to the New South Wales **Eastern Gobbleguts** (*V. novaehollandiae*).

Tailor *Pomatomus saltatrix* TL 1.2m

This voracious hunter of small fishes, especially small pelagics like pilchards, often swims in large formations over coastal reefs. It is a streamlined silvery fish with strong cutting teeth in the jaws. The young enter estuaries, but adults are found mainly in clear coastal waters and spawn offshore. Migrates in large and densely packed schools over long distances along the coast, probably to spawn or following the smaller migrating species on which it feeds. Tailor are widely distributed with populations in the Atlantic, the southern Indian Ocean and eastern Australia, and are a popular game fish with a reputation as a strong fighter.

Yellow-tail Kingfish *Seriola lalandi* TL 2m

A sought-after game fish, mainly schooling offshore but occasionally entering deep harbours or estuaries. Adults are silvery below and dusky greenish grey over the back, and the tail fin is light yellow. Often a broad ochre band runs from the snout to the tail. Juveniles have a

broad-banded pattern of light yellow and grey, and often swim under weed rafts or other large floating objects. The Yellow-tail Kingfish has a maximum weight of 60kg. Prey consist primarily of small pelagic fishes. Broadly distributed in subtropical to temperate seas in the northern and southern hemispheres.

Rainbow Runner *Elagatis bipinnulata* TL 1.2m

This streamlined pelagic species, which sometimes approaches divers, is easily identified by the two parallel blue stripes running from head to tail along the sides. A fast swimmer, usually in small groups of similar-sized individuals, and regularly swims close to reefs to hunt small schooling pelagic fishes. They follow other schooling pelagic hunters to pick up leftovers or join in feeding sprees. Rainbow Runners swim mainly in open seas offshore, but regularly enter deep inshore waters between reefs and can be seen anywhere from the surface to depths of about 20m near the bottom. This species is circumglobal, wide-ranging in tropical seas.

Southern Yellowtail Scad *Trachurus novaezelandiae* TL 30–50cm

A slender trevally-like fish with a yellow tail fin. The very similar **Jack Mackerel** (*T. declivisi*) lacks the yellow tail and has a smaller and more defined black spot behind the head. This species is more oceanic and forms large, dense schools. Both species feed primarily mid-water on zooplankton and form an important part of the food chain followed by the larger pelagic fishes. The Southern Yellowtail Scad is one of the most abundant fishes in southern waters, often forming great schools in coastal bays and harbours, sometimes driven into sheltered bays by the larger pelagic hunters such as tunas.

Big-eye Trevally *Caranx sexfasciatus* TL 85cm

An important food fish, also known as Big-eye Jack. Slender species with a large eye and distinct white tips on the dorsal and anal fins. Small juveniles have a yellowish tail and are inshore, swimming in small groups, becoming more numerous with growth and schools moving to coastal bays. At about 30cm in length they swim in large schools that move along shallow reef slopes, usually staying in an area until they gain confidence to travel in a more pelagic mode. Very large individuals are often seen in small aggregations and sometimes swim solitary. One of the most common tropical trevallies.

White Trevally *Pseudocaranx dentex* TL 80–94cm

Adults are deep-bodied, plain silvery grey with a small dark spot above the gill opening. Juveniles often display a yellow line along their sides, running from the head on to the tail. They are primarily plankton feeders, chasing crustaceans to the surface. When in schools, they cause a

ripple on the surface that is quickly recognised by seabirds looking for an easy feed. The White Trevally is the only large temperate trevally species commonly observed in coastal bays and harbours. The smaller **Skipjack Trevally** (*P. wrighti*) appears to be restricted to temperate Australian waters. Northern populations appear to be a different species.

Melbourne Silver Belly *Parequula melbournensis* TL 18cm

This deep-bodied silvery fish has a pointed, slightly turned-down snout. It is an Australian endemic and the only silver belly species in temperate waters. This genus is easily separated from the tropical species (genus *Gerres*) by the low spines in the front of the dorsal fin instead of being elongated and forming an elevated section. Like other silver bellies, they typically swim in loose groups, feeding from the bottom and following other large fish or rays that disturb the bottom to grab the small invertebrates that are exposed from the sand. They are commonly found on sand and rubble bottom along reef margins in depths to 100m but also enter estuaries and are often seen in the shallows under jetties.

Night

69

Monocle Bream *Scolopsis bilineata* TL 20cm

The Monocle Bream, a type of spinecheek, features a prominent spine below the eye, and shows little colour variation except as a juvenile. Adults have a distinctive double line that runs from below the eye and curves up towards the end of the dorsal fin. In Australia, juveniles are strongly striped over the top with black and yellow to look like the venomous harptail blennies. They occur on rubble and sand from shallow coastal reefs to sheltered reef lagoons. Juveniles are solitary and adults often in pairs. Diet comprises various invertebrates taken from the bottom. The most common and widespread species in the tropical Indo-Pacific.

Big-eye Emperor *Monotaxis grandoculis* TL 60cm

This species has a bulky head featuring large round eyes. Adults are shiny silvery on the sides and dusky over the back. Juveniles are similar in shape, but with a proportionally much larger eye, thin white lines across the back, a grey body and a deeply forked tail fin. Juveniles swim like spinecheeks on rubble patches of reef, stopping suddenly to inspect the bottom for possible prey. Solitary on coastal reefs and in outer reef lagoons. Adults are nocturnal, moving out over the open bottom at night to feed. Only a single species in the genus, which is widespread and common in the tropical Indo-Pacific.

Small-tooth Emperor *Lethrinus microdon* TL 70cm

This fish is often accompanied by fishes such as wrasses that hope to pick up an easy feed. A long-snouted emperor species that is easily recognised by the shape of the head, but there is another very similar species called the **Long-snouted Emperor** which is almost indistinguishable underwater. The latter is spotted on the snout, compared to the lined pattern of the Small-tooth Emperor, and usually occurs in small to large aggregations. The Small-tooth Emperor is mainly a coastal species, usually seen solitary on sand and rubble slopes, feeding on bottom invertebrates that are exposed by blowing the sand.

Gold-spot Emperor *Gnathodentex aurolineatus* TL 30cm

This is one of the smallest emperor species and is usually recognised by the large yellow blotch on the body below the end of the dorsal fin. The blotch is normally bright, though the body can vary from plain light grey to very dark or near black. The blotch probably enables the species to stay in visual touch with each other when visibility is poor. Diet comprises primarily small invertebrates filtered from the sand. Often occurs in large schools with hundreds of individuals swimming closely together over sand habitats near reefs in lagoons or along steep walls with large caves.

71

Snapper *Chrysophrys aurata* TL 1.2m

Adults are deep-bodied with a hump on the head. Colour varies from grey-brown to pink or reddish, usually in relation to sex and depth. Small juveniles have bright iridescent spots. At angling size, they usually swim in small loose groups. Large adults often solitary on deep reefs but school when migrating to spawn, entering harbours or protected bays in great numbers. Small solitary juveniles live deep, moving to shallower depths when forming groups. Large adults enter shallow depths at night to feed. Diet comprises bottom invertebrates and fishes. Specimens up to 20kg sought after by anglers in southern Australian and New Zealand waters.

Silver Bream *Acanthopagrus australis* TL 65cm

Most bream species have shiny silvery scales, a deep body and large tail fin, and can weigh up to 4kg. The Silver Bream has a small but distinct black spot on top of the pectoral fin base, and the lower fins are usually yellow. It is also known simply as Bream or Yellow-finned Bream. There are several bream species distributed along the Australian coast. They are coastal, and juveniles are inshore in estuaries and often in freshwater run-offs. The Silver Bream is the common New South Wales fish, but in Queensland its range overlaps with several similar tropical species.

Oblique-banded Sweetlips *Plectorhinchus lineatus* TL 60cm

Adults are distinctly striped, with the lines angled upwards along the back. Juveniles have horizontal stripes and are difficult to tell from other striped juveniles without knowing the finer details. Juveniles live solitary among boulders or large open corals in coastal waters of lagoons to depths of about 10m. Adults are usually seen in small groups but form schools in some areas. They prefer deep water and when in the shallows, they usually stay adjacent to deep slopes or reef walls. At night, they move out over open bottom to feed on benthic creatures. This species is widespread in the tropical Indo-Pacific.

Slate Sweetlips *Diagramma labiosum* TL 1m

When approached, juveniles wave their tail frantically. Adults have thick fleshy lips and are dull grey, often with a blotched pattern on their sides. Juveniles are distinctively striped and easily recognised by the tall dorsal fin just behind the head. Small juveniles are

solitary and settle on sand or mud, sometimes in a hollowed-out depression. Large juveniles are often in small groups. Adults congregate on deep reefs during the day, moving out at night to feed on open sandflats adjacent to reefs. Mainly a common coastal species, adults ranging to sheltered and deep inner reef habitat and juveniles are inshore, entering shallow estuaries.

73

Red Emperor *Lutjanus sebae* TL 1m

The Red Emperor is a kind of tropical snapper. Large adults are plain red all over. Juveniles have black and white banding which fades with increasing size. By the time their colouration has changed to red, they have moved to deep water. Juveniles are commonly observed in coastal waters, swimming between the spines of sea-urchins when small. Sometimes found in small groups where the urchins congregate on

the open bottom. Adults are thought to form large schools that swim over vast areas, and are reported as good eating. Widespread in the tropical Indo-Pacific, but only juveniles known from southernmost part of its range.

Spanish Flag Snapper *Lutjanus carponotatus* TL 40cm

This tropical snapper species has a distinctive pattern of broad yellow to brown bands along the upper half of the body and slightly faded ones below, usually separating the upper and lower half by a light mid-lateral band from the tip of the snout to the base of the tail fin. Juveniles are similar to adults but with fewer and thicker bands. Tropical snappers form a large family, comprising many groups of similar species. This is a mainly a coastal species. Juveniles live on shallow and heavily vegetated reefs, feeding on benthic invertebrates and small fishes. The Spanish Flag Snapper is widespread in the tropical Indo-Pacific.

Blue-stripe Snapper *Lutjanus kasmira* TL 35cm

 This species is distinctive, with its bright yellow colour and four iridescent blue stripes, and separated from the similar **Five-line Snapper** (*L. quinquelineatus*) which has an extra line along the belly. Juveniles are pale whitish yellow and often have a large diffused black spot on their sides below the end of the dorsal fin. In some areas it swims in large schools, hovering closely together during the day and spreading out at night to feed. Diet comprises small invertebrates and fishes. Juveniles form small groups on rocky reefs in shallow coastal bays and estuaries. Adults range from inshore to outer reefs and offshore reefs, and occur in many oceanic locations. The Blue-stripe Snapper is one of the most widespread and common species in the tropical Indo-Pacific.

Robust Fusilier *Caesio cuning* TL 25–30cm

A deep-bodied fusilier, but streamlined with a large yellow forked tail fin. Blue horizontal bands on the head and a red eye. It has a distinctive colouration with blue and yellow, but could be confused with the **Southern Fusilier** (*Paracaesio xanthurus*), a widespread deepwater snapper with the same body colouration that lives in relatively shallow waters in New South Wales. It is not as deep-bodied as the Robust Fusilier and has a white eye and small scales. Robust Fusilier school in coastal waters, especially around islands near the shore. The Southern Fusilier commonly ranges south to the Solitary Islands of New South Wales.

Gold-band Fusilier *Caesio caerulaurea* TL 25cm

This species is best recognised by the dark streaks in the tail fin and the broad dusky-golden band running from above the eye to above the tail-fin base. Like other fusiliers, it forms large schools but prefers coastal and protected inner reefs, swimming

along reef margins in shallow depths to about 15m. When feeding on zooplankton the schools spread out over large areas and the entire water column. Small juveniles are often solitary and stay close to reefs. They hide in small crevices when approached, enter harbours and often mix with other schooling fishes. A common and widespread tropical Indo-Pacific species.

Black-spot Goatfish *Parupeneus signatus* TL 50cm

 One of the largest Australian goatfishes. Adults have a distinctive black spot on the tail, just behind the dorsal fin. Juveniles are similar to adults, although very large adults become spotted or have blue scribbles all over and fins are often sky-blue. Juveniles in small groups in sheltered coastal bays around rocky reefs, and adults mainly in deeper parts of estuaries or offshore, either solitary or in groups. Feed on the bottom, digging with their strong chin barbels for invertebrates, especially soft-bodied creatures such as worms. An Australian species ranging to New Zealand. Common in New South Wales waters.

Yellow-saddle Goatfish *Parupeneus cyclostomus* TL 38cm

 This species is often noted because of its obvious colour. The bright yellow noted in the young sometimes remains in adults. The normally blue-grey adults feature a large yellow saddle below the end of the dorsal fin. Juveniles are often with other goatfish juveniles and are found accompanied by wrasses, especially of the genus *Thalassoma*, which look for an easy meal when the goatfishes are digging in the bottom. Adults form their own small groups and can be found on shallow reef-flats in coastal waters. Common on coastal reef slopes to outer reef crests, the Yellow-saddle Goatfish is widespread in the tropical Indo-Pacific.

Common Bullseye *Pempheris multiradiata* TL 22cm

Adult

The single angular dorsal fin in the middle of the back and the deep body shape are distinctive features of bullseyes. In addition they have large eyes, and the lateral line comprising scales with sensitive pressure sensors runs all the way to the end of the tail. Most species are dull greyish brown and difficult to identify. Some have black tips or edges on the fins. The Common Bullseye has yellow and black-tipped ventral fins when young, but adults are plain and show more-or-less distinctive banding along the scale rows. Their large mouth is used to secure small planktonic prey at night. This temperate species lives in various habitats from shallow silty reefs inshore to deep clearwater caves offshore, forming schools during the day. It is restricted to Australian waters.

Juvenile

Silver Sweep *Scorpis lineolata* TL 25cm

Sweep are usually plain silvery on their sides, and grey or greenish on top. The top and bottom profiles are almost mirror-like. The soft part of the dorsal fin opposite the identically shaped anal fin and tail fin is deeply forked. The Silver Sweep is a very common species on

coastal reefs, ranging to submerged reefs deep offshore, and usually forming great schools feeding high above reefs on all kinds of plankton, including algae. At night they seek shelter in reefs. Small juveniles are found inshore and often in small schools around jetty pylons and commonly in rockpools.

Brassy Drummer *Kyphosus vaigiensis* TL 50cm

Drummers are related to sweep but are more solid and elongate. The Brassy Drummer has low fins, and each scale has a silvery centre that forms longitudinal lines along the body, straight below and angular above the lateral line. The similar **Snubnose Drummer** (*K. cinerascens*) has elevated dorsal and anal fins forming

angular shapes at the ends. The **Silver Drummer** (*K. sydneyanus*) is plain silvery with a dusky tail. Drummers have a small nibbler-type mouth. Brassy Drummers occur commonly in small groups in coastal and protected inner reef habitats where they feed on plankton. Most species are widespread in the tropical Indo-Pacific.

79

Zebra Fish *Girella zebra* TL 40–54cm

Adult

Adult Zebra Fish are easily identified by their black and white banded body and yellow fins. Juveniles are often dull grey with less distinct banding and can be confused with the juvenile **Luderick** or **Blackfish** (*G. tricuspidata*), a common New South Wales species ranging to South Australia, which is grey with thin dark vertical lines. Adult Zebra Fish form small to large groups, often in very shallow water where they live in deep ledges, and are rather flighty and difficult to approach. In deeper water they swim more openly on reefs and seem less worried about divers. Diet comprises mainly algae that is nibbled from rocks or when suspended and floating in currents. Juveniles are often in rockpools, and adults occur commonly in coastal bays. Zebra Fish are only found in southern Australian waters.

Juvenile

Footballer Sweep *Neatypus obliquus* TL 23cm

This very active fish is easily recognised by the unusual pattern of oblique banding of yellow and white. Usually they form small to large groups when feeding on suspended matter well above the bottom. They also feed in small groups on the bottom itself, moving along quickly. When one individual discovers something, everyone quickly joins in on the activity. Usually seen in depths of 10m or more, and adults are reported to 200m, but sometimes they rise to the surface in turbulent waters around rocky shores to feed on suspended algae or plankton. Mainly common in southern Western Australia.

Stripey *Microcanthus strigatus* TL 16cm

There are two separate populations in Australia, divided between east and west coasts, and a third in the northern Pacific. Easily recognised by shape and striped pattern of yellow and black running at slight angle downward from head to tail. Yellow colour variable from almost white to bright hues, usually darkest above and lightest on the belly. Small juveniles are found mainly inshore in shallow protected coastal waters and sometimes in large rockpools. Adults form schools and hang around rocky ledges with sea-urchins or swim below large rock overhangs or coral plates in various habitats from rocky estuaries to offshore reefs. This species is particularly common north of Sydney.

Mado *Atypichthys strigatus* TL 25cm

A familiar sight to New South Wales reef divers. Mado have a distinctive pattern of thick dark-grey and white stripes and light yellow fins, showing no variation with growth. They feed on almost anything, including algae and plankton, and hang around large predators to feed on the leftovers or suspended bits. Juvenile Mado are mainly found inshore, living in shallow protected waters and in large rockpools. Often abundant on coastal reefs and in estuaries but ranging to moderate depths on offshore reefs. Numbers decrease rapidly in the Bass Strait region, which is the most southern part of the range.

Moonlighter *Tilodon sexfasciatus* TL 35–40cm

Although closely related to the Mado and Stripey, the small juvenile Moonlighter looks more like a butterflyfish with its round, coin-shaped body and the eye-like spots at the end of the dorsal and anal fins. Solitary and secretive on reefs, also like butterfly-fishes. Adults form pairs like many butterflyfishes do, and swim along reefs whilst feeding on bottom invertebrates. Usually lives deep in Victoria but shallow in South Australia below jetties, but juveniles are often found just below the tidal zone. Mainly a coastal species found near reefs and holed up in caves and ledges, usually occurring in small numbers.

Beaked Coralfish *Chelmon rostratus* TL 20cm

The mouth is long, beak- or pincer-like to pick prey from narrow crevices. This species is easily recognised by the broad orange banding over the body and the thinner bands over the head bordered with thin black stripes. Small juveniles are secretive on shallow coastal reefs in protected bays and estuaries. Adults on coastal reefs and in lagoons, usually forming pairs that swim closely together when looking for food. Diet comprises small invertebrates and worms. The species is widespread in the tropical west Pacific but is mainly confined to mainland regions and with a patchy distribution. Locally, it occurs in abundance.

Rainford's Butterflyfish *Chaetodon rainfordi* TL 16cm

This coral-associated species includes coral polyps as an important part of its diet and is not found where corals are absent. It is distinctively coloured, with the bright yellow deep body and broad grey vertical bands bordered thickly with orange. Juveniles are similar to adults. Juveniles live secretively in branching corals and adults swim about openly, usually in pairs. The similar and closely related **Gold-banded Butterflyfish** (*C. aureofasciatus*) sometimes hybridises with Rainford's Butterflyfish. Locally common on sheltered inner reef zones. An Australian endemic species, it is mainly confined to Queensland with juveniles ranging to northern New South Wales.

Saddled Butterflyfish *Chaetodon ephippium* TL 24cm

A distinctively and beautifully coloured butterflyfish with a large black area above the white curving band that runs from below the spinous part of the dorsal fin to the top of the tail-fin base. Adults have a long trailing filament on the dorsal fin. Juveniles live secretively in shallow rocky reefs in protected coastal bays and have a rounded dorsal fin without the trailing filament. Adults pair and are usually seen on shallow reef-flats in clear water on outer reefs, rarely deeper than 20m. Feeds on a variety of bottom invertebrates, especially small tubeworms. This species is widespread in the tropical Indo-Pacific.

Threadfin Butterflyfish *Chaetodon auriga* TL 24cm

Easily recognised by its white body ending in bright yellow, with a black band over the eye, and pattern of thin angular lines. Usually a distinct black spot on the dorsal fin. Juveniles range into subtropical waters as larvae are carried south and are some of the first butterflyfishes to settle in summer in the Sydney area, staying close to ledges with sea-urchins. Feeds on bottom-dwelling invertebrates, especially small tubeworms. Adults pair and can be found in habitats from shallow coastal bays and lagoons to moderate depths on outer reefs. Schools in a few oceanic locations. Common and widespread in the tropical Indo-Pacific.

Vagabond Butterflyfish *Chaetodon vagabundus* TL 20cm

Very similar to the **Threadfin Butterflyfish** but lacks the dorsal fin filament as an adult and has black bands along the base of the soft dorsal fin and in the tail fin. Small juveniles have a false eye at the rear of the dorsal fin, and the black line over the end of the body is often bordered with orange. Juveniles are solitary and live

secretively in rocky reefs with sea-urchins. Adults pair on coastal and protected inner reefs but form small groups in some oceanic locations. They feed on small invertebrates. This is a common and widespread tropical Indo-Pacific species.

Dusky Butterflyfish *Chaetodon flavirostris* TL 20cm

This species is easily recognised by the mainly dark-grey body with yellow or orange in the fins and snout all around. Small juveniles have a false eye spot on the rear end of the dorsal fin, and live secretively in coastal reefs with rocky ledges, and usually with sea-urchins in the Sydney area. Large adults form pairs and prefer the clearer coastal and off-shore reefs. Juveniles are solitary and very territorial, claiming a small patch of reef.

This east coast species ranges well into the tropical south Pacific. Adults are common in northern New South Wales, occasionally ranging south to Sydney.

Gunther's Butterflyfish *Chaetodon guentheri* TL 14cm

The least secretive or shy butterflyfish in Australian waters. Easily identified by the white colour and fine black spotting. Tiny juveniles settle in rocky ledges but soon swim about in small groups. Adults form large schools in some areas and often swim high above the bottom in open water where they feed on zooplankton but also actively clean parasites from pelagic fishes. On the bottom they usually travel in small groups or pairs. This species occurs throughout the west Pacific but in equatorial waters only deep, preferring cooler sponge areas. Adults range well south in New South Wales, but are usually offshore.

Blue-dash Butterflyfish *Chaetodon plebeius* TL 12cm

This species is coral-dependent, feeding on the polyps. The bright yellow-coloured body, with a blue dash like it has been brushed on, easily identifies this species. Small juveniles have a large eye-like spot on the tail-fin base. Small juveniles are only found amongst the close-set branches of

branching coral plates. Adults usually swim about openly in pairs over the coral areas. It is a common Australian species found from inshore to protected outer reef habitats that ranges along the east coast of New Guinea, north to southern Japan in the west Pacific, and to Fiji in the central Pacific.

86

Chevroned Butterflyfish *Chaetodon trifascialis* TL 14cm

The elongated body and close-set chevroned black stripes on the white body are diagnostic for the species. Small juveniles are black over the back end of the body and have a clear tail fin. They live secretively inside densely branching corals. Adults have a mostly black tail fin and often pair, swimming openly about but staying close to the large coral plates they associate with. They feed on the coral polyps and are coral-dependent, usually not doing well in captivity. They inhabit coastal and offshore outer reefs where suitable corals grow. This species is widespread and common in the tropical Indo-Pacific.

Long-nose Butterflyfish *Forcipiger flavissimus* TL 22cm

This is the most common of two very similar species that are easily recognised by the mostly bright yellow body and exceptionally long beak-like snout. The juvenile Long-nose Butterflyfish lives solitary, and adults often pair. They feed on small invertebrates but also pick at the larger sea-urchins where they can reach edible parts with their snout. They can be found in shallow depths as well as deep, and live in various habitats from coastal reefs and lagoons to reef walls. The species is widespread in the tropical Indo-Pacific and expatriates into subtropical zones.

87

Reef Bannerfish *Heniochus acuminatus* TL 25cm

The Reef Bannerfish is one of two almost identical fishes with distinctive black and white banding and a long wimple-like white extension on the dorsal fin. The Reef Bannerfish and the **Schooling Bannerfish** (*H. diphreutes*) are both common in Australian waters, but only experts can tell them apart. However, the Reef Bannerfish pairs as an adult and feeds on small invertebrates on the bottom, whilst the Schooling Bannerfish forms large schools to feed on zooplankton. The other differences are obvious only when the two species are next to each other. Bannerfishes feature a long extended dorsal fin spine with a broad white-coloured membrane seen in few other fishes; only the well-known **Moorish Idol** (*Zanclus cornutus*) shares this in Australian waters. Juvenile bannerfishes are found inshore in protected bays where they usually form small groups. Adults occur inshore, as well as offshore in various depths.

In formation

Half-circled Angelfish *Pomacanthus semicirculatus* TL 35cm

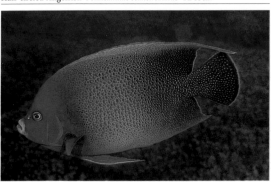

This angelfish starts off with rounded fins and a few white and blue lines which become more numerous with age until it acquires the complicated adult pattern and long, pointed fins. The backward spine from the gill cover, bright blue in adults, is used in territorial and other disputes. Small juveniles are secretive and inhabit the back of very shallow rocky ledges, feeding on the algae growing along the front. Adults prefer the deeper coastal reef slopes and drop-offs, usually swimming by themselves and often in the open. Widespread in the tropical Indo-Pacific, but only juveniles range to subtropical zones in summer months.

Emperor Angelfish *Pomacanthus imperator* TL 38cm

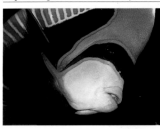

Juveniles bear no resemblance to the adult. The complicated pattern of the young confuses possible predators. However, juveniles are often seen cleaning large fishes and perhaps the pattern serves to recognise this behaviour. Juveniles live deep, usually below 25m, isolated in sponges on open bottom slopes. Unlike their close relatives, juveniles of this angelfish are not known to occur outside the breeding range. This suggests a different behaviour of the pelagic stage, perhaps as they live deep rather than near the surface. Adults are mainly found in cave areas along reef walls. Widespread in the tropical Indo-Pacific, and the range shown applies to the adult.

89

Scribbled Angelfish *Chaetodontoplus duboulayi* TL 25cm

An Australian endemic species with a distinctive colour pattern of grey and blue scribbles all over the body and a broad yellow band over the head just behind the eye. Juveniles and adults are very similar in colour and shape. Males are more elongated than females. Mainly a coastal reef fish in protected areas where they feed on a variety of algae, invertebrates and, especially, sponges. Juveniles are solitary and secretive among boulders or in ledges. Adults swim about openly and form pairs or small groups and can be approached at close range. The species is common throughout its range.

Blue and Gold Angelfish *Centropyge bicolor* TL 12–16cm

The yellow and blue pattern changes abruptly about halfway along the body. A large spine protrudes backwards at the corner of the gill plate below the eye. Small juveniles are solitary and very secretive in narrow rocky crevices or behind corals. Adults are very active, forming small groups led by a large male, swimming on reef crests to feed on algae grazed from the flat surfaces of rocks or dead corals. They occur on coastal reefs as well as in protected parts of outer reefs. This popular aquarium fish is common throughout the tropical west Pacific. Juveniles range into subtropical waters in the summer months.

Keyhole Angelfish *Centropyge tibicen* TL 15cm

The white blotch on the jet-black body identifies this quick-moving species. The white area varies from a thin vertical bar to an area almost one-third of its body size. Tiny juveniles frequent rocky ledges with sea-urchins during the summer in the Sydney area. The yellow band along the anal fin only develops in adults, and large individuals may have a blue sheen all over the body. Juveniles live solitary, and adults form loose groups, staying close to the bottom. Occurs inshore on reefs and under jetties, as well as on outer rocky reefs, and in mixed algae and coral habitats. This is a tropical Indo-Pacific species.

Regal Angelfish *Pygoplites diacanthus* TL 25cm

This multicoloured species, with vertical orange, white and blue bands, is common on rich coral reefs, often along steep walls in large caves with rich sponge growth on clear coastal to outer reefs. Small juveniles are very secretive in the back of caves. They are similar to adults but have only a few broad vertical

bands and a large false eye mark at the rear end of the dorsal fin. Adults are very active during the day, swimming about openly, and often several individuals can be seen close together under coral plates. Only a single wide-ranging species is recognised in the tropical Indo-Pacific.

91

Tall-fin Batfish *Platax teira* TL 45–60cm

This species goes through great changes in the shape of the fins. Juvenile batfishes are unusual in having very tall vertical fins supported by a small coin-like round body. Adults become a solid rounded fish with proportionally much shorter fins. Although only five batfish species occur commonly in the tropical Indo-Pacific, each with a distinctive shape or colour, confusion persists throughout the literature on their correct common or scientific name. The Tall-fin Batfish is the most common species. It has the highest dorsal fin as a juvenile, and adults are easily recognised by the black spot below the pectoral fin. Juveniles float in coastal waters on the surface with debris from rivers, and adults move to deep water and occur inshore as well as offshore. They are often seen solitary but occasionally form large schools on remote reefs or shipwrecks.

Long-snout Boarfish *Pentaceropsis recurvirostris* TL 50cm

This unusually shaped species is easily recognised by the long snout and fin shapes. It is attractive and distinctive, being pure white with a few black spots, and has tall dorsal fin spines with feathery membranes. Generally it lives on deep reefs and is often seen on shipwrecks, sometimes in loose groups. It has an exceptional depth range, being known as deep as 260m, and also enters very shallow depths in sheltered bays. Large individuals are often inquisitive and follow divers. Juveniles appear to be restricted to deep water and are rarely seen. Adults occur commonly on Australia's southern coast and are well known to divers there.

Large adult

Old Wife *Enoplosus armatus* TL 25cm

Adults

A unique Australian species, placed in its own family. It is easily recognised by shape and colour, especially the tall double dorsal fin and zebra-like pattern. The spines in the dorsal fin are venomous. Adults occur in large schools but form individual pairs that separate temporarily from the school when getting ready to spawn. Tiny juveniles live in seagrass beds and look nothing like the adult, missing the tall dorsal fin and being almost black. They soon develop the fins and familiar Old Wife pattern, however. The larger juveniles stay close to weedy or algae-covered reefs. Feeds on small crustaceans and zooplankton. Mainly a coastal species, preferring still waters in protected bays or deep offshore reefs. One of the best known common fishes in southern waters.

Small juvenile

Magpie Perch *Cheilodactylus nigripes* TL 40cm

A species of morwong, easily recognised by colour with broad black and white vertical banding at all stages. Large adults can change colour quickly, usually reversing the second black band to white and the normally white central space to grey. Adults occur in small loose groups on deeper reefs in coastal bays and are often seen feeding for small invertebrates by filtering mouthfuls of sand through the gills. Small juveniles live solitary in shallow protected bays with rocks and weed adjacent to sand and rubble from which they feed. This species is common on the southern coast of Australia and is also known in New Zealand waters.

Bastard Trumpeter *Latridopsis forsteri* TL 65cm

A close relative of morwongs, which is most evident in the larval and postlarval stages. Adults are mainly grey, sometimes with a bronze hue over the back. Juveniles enter shallow bays, but adults are mainly coastal on deeper reefs where they school. The closely related **Striped**

Trumpeter (*Latris lineata*) grows about twice as long and is mainly confined to Tasmania and the Bass Strait region. The much smaller **Real-bastard Trumpeter** (*Mendosoma lineatum*) is restricted in Australia to Tasmanian waters. Generally common, and very large schools occur in deep offshore waters as they migrate along the coast. Restricted to temperate waters.

Southern Seacarp *Aplodactylus arctidens* TL 65cm

A member of a small temperate group of Southern Hemisphere fishes, most of which are found in Australian waters. They are robust, elongated fishes with a large notched dorsal fin and a short-based anal fin. The Southern Seacarp typically congregate on reefs in the path of tidal currents and feed on floating algae or weeds coming past. They are sloppy swimmers and spend most of the time lying on the bottom on weed-covered rocks. Juveniles are secretive amongst boulders in the same areas as the adults. The Southern Seacarp is common in the Bass Strait region.

Coral Hawkfish *Cirrhitichthys falco* TL 65mm

Hawkfishes are typified by the small tufts in the dorsal fin spines. They are best identified by the colour pattern on the body. The body is usually white, and the spots and blotches are red and arranged in saddle-like bands over the back. They occur on clear coastal to outer reef crests where they perch themselves between rocks or corals using their large pectoral fins. They feed on a variety of small invertebrates and fishes during the day. The Coral Hawkfish is one of the most commonly observed species on coral reefs. Most species are widespread in the tropical Indo-Pacific.

Ring-eyed Hawkfish *Paracirrhites arcatus* TL 14cm

The head of this species has peculiar and brightly coloured lines circling the area behind the eye and a series of dashes of the same colours along the edge of the gill-plate. The body colour is variable from greenish or yellowish grey to reddish, and often has a thick white stripe below the end of the

dorsal fin. Like most hawkfishes, it typically perches on its pectoral fins at a high point on the reef. It feeds on small invertebrates and fishes during the day. It commonly lives in loose groups on outer reefs with rich coral growth. A widespread species in the tropical Indo-Pacific.

Longnose Hawkfish *Oxycirrhites typus* TL 10cm

The Longnose Hawkfish is readily recognised by the unusual very long snout and elongated body. Colour is almost white, and the body has thin red lines that form a pattern of squares. They typically live along outer reef walls on Gorgonians and Black Coral where they are well-camouflaged. They regularly move position, sometimes hovering between the branches of the corals checking for prey. The Longnose Hawkfish feeds actively all day on small invertebrates and zooplankton drifting past and coming within reach. It is a widespread tropical Indo-Pacific species. In Australia it is primarily found on the outer Great Barrier Reef.

Scalyfin *Parma victoriae* TL 25cm

These are called scalyfins as the scales covering the body extend well on to the fins, but they are a kind of damselfish. Adults are generally drab, but juveniles are bright orange with iridescent blue lines over the head and back. An aggressive and territorial species. The male clears a rock surface for a nesting site and guards the eggs. The Scalyfin feeds primarily on small invertebrates. This temperate genus with fewer than ten species is confined to Australian and New Zealand waters. The Scalyfin is very common on shallow reefs in bays to deep offshore in southern Victoria.

Immaculate Damsel *Mecaenichthys immaculatus* TL 15cm

Closely related to scalyfins, but less aggressive, and adults and juveniles are often found together in the same areas. Adults are silvery and light grey, and fins light blue. Juveniles are brightly coloured in yellow or orange and with thick iridescent blue lines along the back. They

feed on small invertebrates from rocks and sand. Found in protected coastal bays and rocky reefs, especially in large boulder areas clear of large weeds or kelp, where they swim near the sandy or rubble bottom. Only one species in the genus and restricted to Australian waters. Mainly common off southern New South Wales.

Scissor-tail Sergeant *Abudefduf sexfasciatus* TL 15cm

Sergeant are typically banded. The Scissor-tail Sergeant is best identified by the dark streaks in the tail fin from the base to the end of the pointed lobes. Juveniles swim well away from or above reefs in shallow coastal bays to feed on plankton matter and range far south along Australian coasts during the summer months when larvae are carried by the currents. Sometimes small juveniles are found out at sea with floating weeds. Adults prefer a clear offshore or outer reef habitat and school on protected reef-flats. The species is widespread and common in the tropical Indo-Pacific.

Royal Damsel *Neoglyphidodon melas* TL 15cm

Juveniles are beautifully coloured with bright yellow backs and blue on the lower fins, but adults become a drab all-black fish. The juvenile is solitary and very territorial. It typically lives on shallow reef crests where there is rich soft-coral growth and often it can be seen from a distance as it shows itself high above the bottom looking out for zooplankton drifting past. Adults form small loose aggregations on coastal reef slopes with gutters and channels. This species usually occurs in small numbers on shallow reefs in depths of between about 3 and 15m. It is widespread in the tropical west Pacific.

One-spot Puller *Chromis hypsilepis* TL 15cm

A familiar fish to New South Wales divers, it occurs abundantly on offshore reefs, often clouding the water column when feeding above the bottom on zooplankton. It is a plain bluish grey fish with a distinctive white spot at the end of the dorsal fin. The One-spot Puller is a community spawner, and these activities are

phased with the moon. Parents congregate along rock walls where they lay and guard their eggs. Juveniles are commonly found on shallow estuarine rocky reefs. It is primarily a New South Wales species that ranges far south as larvae drift down in currents.

Blue Damsel *Pomacentrus coelestis* TL 85mm–10cm

These iridescent fishes sparkle in the sunlight, seemingly advertising their presence. Commonly brilliantly blue, but there are some geographical variations, often with a yellow anal fin. This photograph was taken in New South Wales. Adults form small groups on rubble reef in sandy areas where they dig their own holes for

shelter and spawning sites. Small juveniles settle on rocky coastal reefs in ledges and amongst small boulders where there are lots of sea-urchins. One of the most widespread and common species of blue damsel, and one of the first tropicals to settle in southern New South Wales during summer.

Humbug *Dascyllus aruanus* TL 8cm

Adults

The Humbug is distinctly banded with black and white, but the very similar though less common **Black-tail Humbug** (*D. melanurus*) could easily be overlooked if insufficient notice is taken of detail. As the name suggests, it has a mostly black tail and sometimes swims mixed with the Humbug. Humbugs congregate in small coral outcrops where they can seek refuge among the branches and are found mainly in sheltered lagoons where they feed above the bottom on zooplankton drifting past. Tiny juveniles are sometimes noted amongst the spines of sea-urchins. They are found inshore, as well as on outer reefs. This is a common and widespread species in the tropical Indo-Pacific.

Juvenile, Sydney

Barrier Reef Anemonefish *Amphiprion akindynos* TL 11cm

A damselfish that lives in association with anemones. This brown species has thin white lines, adults with one over the head and middle of the body and young with an additional one on the tail. Adults usually live in pairs, and juveniles are often present in the same host anemone. Eggs usually laid against dead coral in reach of the anemone and cared for by parents. On the Great Barrier Reef it lives with host anemone in shallow lagoons and protected parts of outer and inner reefs to about 25m depth. An Australian endemic species confined to the east coast and common throughout its range.

Spine-cheek Anemonefish *Premnas biaculeatus* TL 15cm

This species has a large spine on the cheek that is clearly visible in the large adults where it passes the white head band. It is variable in colour, ranging from bright orange to dark red or brown. The thin white bands usually encircle the body. Mainly found in pairs on coastal reefs and in protected inner reef areas. The pairs usually comprise a large female and a much smaller male. This species associates with only one species of anemone that is usually positioned well down into the reef so it is protected from surrounding hard corals. Broadly distributed in the tropical Indo-Pacific.

Eastern Blue Groper *Achoerodus viridis* TL 1.2m

This groper is actually a kind of wrasse. Like most wrasses, the juvenile and sexes have different colour phases. Small juveniles are green and usually found in seagrass beds. Females are reddish brown with a series of pale spots, and males vary from grey to bright blue. It is common in New South Wales where blue gropers are befriended by divers. They often patiently follow divers at close range, in search of an easy feed of crushed sea-urchin. Juveniles occur inshore, and adults venture into deep water offshore. Subtropical species ranging into temperate zones.

Coral Hogfish *Bodianus axillaris* TL 20cm

This fish goes through an amazingly quick and dramatic colour change from juvenile to adult. The juvenile is jet-black with a series of pure white spots, and this pattern can remain until adult size and even remains in some females. It only takes about a week to change completely to the other phase that shows no resemblance to the first phase. The Coral Hogfish lives on coastal to outer reefs and juveniles are often deep on rocky reefs in small caves, sometimes cleaning other fishes. It occurs widespread throughout the tropical Indo-Pacific, and juveniles range into subtropical zones during summer months.

103

Harlequin Tuskfish *Choerodon fasciatus* TL 25cm

Tuskfishes derived their name from their canine-like teeth, used to crush shrimps or crabs. This species is easily identified by the red bands over the body and head. Juveniles have light-brown bands with narrow grey interspaces and false eye spots in the fins. Adults swim openly over the rubble bottom on inner reefs and shelter in large caves or overhangs. Small juveniles are secretive and stay in the shade of the reef, usually swimming on vertical walls or upside down on the ceilings of caves. The Harlequin Tuskfish is primarily a common Queensland species.

Banded Maori *Cheilinus fasciatus* TL 35cm

Maori wrasses are named after the scribbled cheek patterns of the adults, which resemble the face paintings of the New Zealand Maori people. Large males of the Banded Maori are bright orange or red on the head. Juveniles and females are brown to black and white banded, with white as narrow interspaces in small juveniles. Adults swim openly along reefs near sand and rubble zones, often in small loose groups that dart from different directions to investigate disturbances involving possible prey. Small juveniles are secretive in corals. Common on coastal reefs and in protected areas on outer reefs. Widespread in the tropical Indo-Pacific.

Crimson-banded Wrasse *Notolabrus gymnogenis* TL 40cm

An Australian subtropical wrasse that goes through colour changes with growth and varies greatly according to habitat. Males are distinctive in having a bright red dorsal fin and anal fin, and an almost white tail. Females are mainly grey-brown to red-brown with numerous small white spots all over. Juveniles live on rocky reefs with weed or algae coverage and match the colour of the dominating vegetation. Adults range to moderately deep sponge reefs on which the females are reddish-brown. Usually in small groups on shallow protected reefs, ranging to 40m depth. A common New South Wales species.

Senator Wrasse *Pictilabrus laticlavius* TL 25cm

This temperate Australian wrasse has local colour variations that relate to surrounding weeds and algae. In New South Wales the adults are normally bright green, while in Tasmania they are more reddish. Juveniles are plain with small blue spots, usually well-camouflaged by

weeds. They normally occur in small groups. In areas where the species is common, adults swim about openly and are inquisitive towards divers. Primarily a coastal shallow-water species, but often in surge zones and sometimes on sponge reefs to depths of about 30m and around offshore islands. Common on most coastal reefs in the range.

Checkerboard Wrasse *Halichoeres hortulanus* TL 25cm

Juveniles differ considerably from adults, and there are some geographical variations, particularly between the Indian and Pacific oceans. Small juveniles are white with diffused black banding and a yellow-edged false eye spot in the dorsal fin. Adults in the Pacific have two white or yellow saddle-like spots on the back, while Indian Ocean populations have only one. Juveniles are solitary and swim secretively in narrow ledges or amongst small boulders. Adults swim over reef crests from coastal to outer reef zones, with large males keeping an eye on any females in the area. A common and widespread tropical Indo-Pacific species.

Choat's Wrasse *Macropharyngodon choati* TL 11cm

This beautiful wrasse is known only on Australia's east coast. Adults are white and busily coloured with orange blotches all over. Juveniles are white with few orange blotches and have an elevated section on the front of the dorsal fin. They occur commonly on sheltered protected reefs and in large lagoons with mixed coral and algae growth

and usually swim in small aggregations comprising mostly females and one large male. The juveniles are secretive when very small, and are usually solitary on small outcrops of reef or algae on sand to depths of about 20m. Common in southern Queensland.

Black-backed Wrasse *Anampses neoguinaicus* TL 12cm

This is an unusually coloured species. The pale greenish white body with black over the head is very distinctive in juveniles and adult females, which have false eye-spots at the end of the dorsal and anal fins. In males the black is mostly restricted to above the head and there is no eye-spot on the fins. Adults in small loose groups of females with a large male in charge, and juveniles are solitary. They feed on encrusting worms, crushing the calcareous tubes with their chisel-like teeth. Occurs on clear reefs, rarely inshore. Range extends north along eastern New Guinea to southern Japan.

Red-spot Wrasse *Stethojulis bandanensis* TL 14cm

In this genus the sexes look completely different from each other. Females are generally a dull colour with fine spotting. Males have iridescent blue lines running from snout to tail. They swim in loose groups of females with a patrolling male. A shallow-water species, usually on reef-flats in depths of a few metres. Usually the male is noticed as it swims

high above reefs and the bright iridescent blue lines are an eye-catcher. The Red-spot Wrasse is the most common and widespread of a number of similar species, occurring throughout the tropical Indo-Pacific and ranging into subtropical zones.

Maori Wrasse *Ophthalmolepis lineolata* TL 47cm

In large adult males the head is scribbled with blue lines. Mainly brown, white and grey, in broad horizontal bands. Juveniles similar to females. Small juveniles inhabit shallow bays and harbours, but large adults prefer reefs with sponges and other invertebrate growth. Often abundant on reefs in depths of about 30m. They swim over sand or high above the bottom when there is plankton, but usually feed on the bottom. They bury themselves in the sand to sleep, usually picking the same spot every night. This single temperate species is very common in New South Wales and southern Western Australia.

Comb Wrasse *Coris picta* TL 24cm

A distinctive subtropical wrasse. Adults white with a broad black band running from the snout through the eye to the yellow tail. Juveniles similar but lack yellow on the tail fin. They occur in shallow bays in small-boulder reef along the main reef margins on to sand or rubble and quickly bury themselves in the sand when threatened. Large juveniles form small groups, often with large adults. Tiny black and white juveniles clean other fishes. Males are territorial, patrolling large section of reef, and regularly display to females. At night, they sleep buried under the sand. Very common on offshore reefs in southern New South Wales.

Gaimard Wrasse *Coris gaimard* TL 35cm

This species is probably best known from the juvenile stage when it is bright orange or red with a series of white saddles over the back. Adults are completely different but also beautiful, with multicoloured spots and bands and at some stage a bright yellow tail fin. Juveniles are solitary and swim close to the bottom on rubble patches amongst reef. Adults swim over large areas of reef and roll large pieces of rock or coral to get to food underneath. This species occurs in clear coastal reef habitat to outer reefs, and is widespread in the west Pacific.

Moon Wrasse *Thalassoma lunare* TL 22cm

This fish swims mainly with its pectoral fins. Adults are mostly green with a yellow tail, but large males become blue. Small juveniles are solitary but soon form aggregations to hunt small bottom-dwelling invertebrates. Adults often form large groups and are involved with any feeding activities of large fish, swimming boldly with large predators and stealing fish-eggs that are deposited on rock surfaces. Damselfishes guarding their brood are particularly vulnerable when a school of the wrasses discovers their nesting site. The species is very common throughout the tropical Indo-Pacific, ranging into subtropical zones.

Blue-streak Cleaner Wrasse *Labroides dimidiatus* TL 10cm

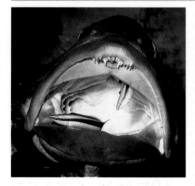

The cleaner wrasse is specially adapted to almost full-time cleaning activities. Small juveniles are black with a thin blue line from the tip of the snout over the top of the tail fin. Adults are pale blue with a black stripe. Cleaner wrasses have a special place on the reef where they serve customers by picking off parasites, cleaning food from teeth or gills, and attending to wounds. Most fish are able to distinguish between the real cleaner and the mimicking blenny (*Aspidontus taeniatus*). Widespread in the tropical Indo-Pacific, but ranges well into subtropical waters where it cleans temperate species of fish.

Cigar Wrasse *Cheilio inermis* TL 48cm

An extremely elongated wrasse, dull in colour though sometimes it is bright yellow. Large males develop an ornamental spot or multiple spots of orange, black, white and yellow just behind the pectoral fin. Juveniles have indistinct longitudinal bands. Swims in groups of females with a patrolling male. Congregates to spawn in phase with the moon. Eggs are pelagic. It feeds on crabs, shrimps, and small sea-urchins and fishes. Common in seagrass beds and on weed-covered reefs but can be found on soft-coral reef tops in coastal waters. Mainly in very shallow depths to 10m, often intertidal. Widespread in the tropical Indo-Pacific.

Rainbow Cale *Odax acroptilus* TL 30cm

Cales are a unique Australian and New Zealand group of fishes that have adapted to a weed environment. The Rainbow Cale is one of the most strikingly coloured species when the male spreads its fins, showing iridescent blue lines combined with a green body. Small juveniles are secretive in seagrasses and dense weeds. Adults swim amongst large weeds and kelp and often rise above to check on a diver, or are seen when swimming between kelp patches. Mainly a coastal species and often in surge or high-energy zones. It is common but hides most of the time.

Blue Weed Whiting *Haletta semifasciata* TL 35cm

This cale is shaped like a whiting and is commonly caught off jetties in bays with seagrasses. Adults are mainly bluish green or brownish with blue markings on the head, but some males are bright metallic blue all over. The young are secretive in seagrass beds, with excellent camouflage: green with a white longitudinal stripe along the body. Adults form large travelling schools that swim through or just above the seagrasses, feeding on small invertebrates, with the blue males often swimming separate from the schools. This species is mainly in coastal bays, including areas affected by the ocean swell. Found only in Australian waters.

Two-colour Parrotfish *Cetoscarus bicolor* TL 90cm

This species has three different stages that look completely different from each other. Tiny juveniles are snow-white with an orange band over the head; females have black spots on white over the body below the lateral line, with brown above; and males are bright green with pink spots and lines over the body, head and fins. Juveniles live solitary in protected bays and lagoons with rich coral growth. Adults form small groups, often of only a single sex, that can be found on slopes and walls from coastal to outer reef habitats. Broadly distributed in the tropical Indo-Pacific.

Surf Parrotfish *Scarus rivulatus* TL 40cm

One of several very similar species and particularly females are difficult to identify underwater. Males have a yellow pectoral fin. When in schools the majority are female. The schools enter very shallow depths on high tide to feed on algae scraped from the corals with their beak-like jaws. Parrotfishes digest a lot of coral bits at the same time and their waste products are an important ingredient in the reef-building process. The Surf Parrotfish is a common Queensland species, mainly found in inshore reefs, often in silty areas, but also on clear outer reefs. It is widespread in the tropical west Pacific.

Yellow-head Parrotfish *Scarus spinus* TL 30cm

Adult

This is a small parrotfish, and males are easily identified by their green body and bright yellow head. Females are dark brown with small white speckles over the body and look similar to a number of other species. Females are usually in small groups and often mix with other species. Males are usually seen alone on reef crests and occasionally mix with the females. An outer reef species sometimes found on clear inner reefs, swimming on shallow reef tops feeding on the bases of coral where algaes grow on the dead areas, and in deep lagoons with rich coral growth. A widespread species in the tropical west Pacific.

Large juvenile

Lyre-tail Grubfish *Parapercis schauinslandi* TL 18cm

Grubfishes perch on the bottom on their ventral fins. This species is pale creamy coloured with red spots or blotches and a yellowish head. Adults have bands of dark saddles and blotches along the body, and often swim high above the bottom to feed on zooplankton. Only adults develop the long lyre-tail fin. Juveniles are usually pale with a few red markings and stay on the bottom to feed. Adults form small groups in feeding areas and pair off in small territories. This grubfish inhabits coastal to outer reefs and usually lives deep on slopes in current-prone areas on rubble bottom. A widespread tropical Indo-Pacific species.

Spotted Grubfish *Parapercis ramsayi* TL 20cm

This distinctive species is restricted to southern Australian waters. Body is bony white and brownish grey over the back with a line of black spots from above the pectoral fin to the upper end of the tail-fin base. Small juveniles have a false eye spot on top of the tail-fin base. Occurs in coastal bays and offshore reefs commonly between 30 and 50m, but enters shallow harbours and juveniles found in a few metres' depth. It lives on sand, fine rubble and mud adjacent to reefs and makes a burrow under solid objects. Common in some areas of New South Wales and South Australia.

Thornfish *Bovichtus angustifrons* TL 28cm

The head carries two large backward-pointing spines, and this species is sometimes confused with dragonets which are similar in shape and have two spines low on the side of the head. Colour is usually reddish, but is highly variable and usually matches the habitat. Thornfishes live in various habitats from coastal and estuarine waters in current-prone areas to deep offshore. Often small groups sit on vertical rock faces and jetty pylons, and juveniles can be found in rockpools. Thornfishes have close affinities with Antarctic fishes and are restricted to Southern Hemisphere temperate zones. Common in Tasmania and Victoria.

Red-streaked Blenny *Cirripectes stigmaticus* TL 10cm

This alert little fish disappears in the corals when approached, but usually reappears soon after to see if it is safe to come out. Adults have bright red streaks over the sides of the body but difficult to recognise underwater. Juveniles are mainly black

or dark brown. This blenny feeds close to its hideout on algae scraped from dead coral. Often it sits on top of the coral to check if it is safe before moving to a feeding site nearby. Occurs on coastal reef crests with rich coral growth, usually in 3 to 6m depth. This species is widespread in the tropical west Pacific.

115

Yellow-lined Harptail Blenny *Meiacanthus lineatus* TL 12cm

This blenny is left alone by most predators as it possesses venomous fangs. Brightly coloured with yellow and black lines over the back. Openly swims over rubble patches on reefs. Some other blennies that are normally a brownish colour take on the same colour pattern when around this fish, and some juvenile Monocle Bream gain protection from wearing this colouration. Adult Yellow-lined Harptail Blenny have long filaments on the tips of the tail fin. It occurs singly or in pairs in clear coastal bays and inner reefs on rubble bottom. Known only in tropical Australian waters and is common in Queensland waters.

Two-colour Combtooth Blenny *Ecsenius bicolor* TL 85mm

Orange form

This elongated species has two distinct colour forms, but its name applies to the half-black, half-orange form. A rarer variety, with black over the entire back and white below, often found in the same area. Such variations may relate to territorial claims. Combtooth blennies have numerous long slender teeth for scraping algae off rocks or dead coral. They hide out in narrow round holes in coral bases, often made by worms, and feed on nearby algae. This species occurs on clear coastal to outer reef crests and slopes with gutters and rubble. It is widespread in the tropical west Pacific.

White form

Tube-worm Blenny *Plagiotremus rhinorynchos* TL 12cm

This fish moves tail-first into empty tube-worm shells which it uses for shelter. A very slender species that varies from black to orange with blue lines and yellow to pale-mauve fins. The mouth is set back from the snout, and it has long fangs which it uses to defend itself. It can give a nasty bite if handled. The head usually sticks out when it is resting in its tube. Males also use the shell for nesting, and entice the female to lay her eggs in the tube by displaying and dancing in front. If successful, the eggs are guarded by the male. Tube-worm Blennies occur on coastal and estuarine reefs to depths of about 15m. A widespread species in the tropical Indo-Pacific.

Johnston's Weedfish *Heteroclinus johnstoni* TL 40cm

Johnston's Weedfish is the largest Australian weedfish. Juveniles are often black- and white-banded, and adults are variable brown and grey with a series of eye-like spots along the base of the dorsal fin. Weedfishes are life-bearers, and most species have a limited and localised distribution as there is no pelagic stage like in most other marine fishes that are dispersed by currents, often over vast distances. All weedfishes live in seagrasses or tall algae-covered reefs. Johnston's Weedfish feeds primarily on shrimps and crabs. Found in shallow bays but also occurs offshore to at least 50m depth. It is a common southern Victorian species.

Golden Weedfish *Cristiceps aurantiacus* TL 18cm

This weedfish has a very tall first dorsal fin. Adults are yellow to golden brown, usually with a few small white spots along the base of the dorsal fin and mid-line of body and a dark stripe vertically over the head, running from the eye down. Juveniles are

usually pale whitish yellow with pink markings, showing faint barring. Golden Weedfish are life-bearers. Mostly live in kelp when adult, but are sometimes found on sand gutters with loose weeds, well away from reefs, and reported to a depth of 60m. This is primarily a New South Wales species.

Fingered Dragonet *Dactylopus dactylopus* TL 18cm

Adult

The back of this fish is sandy coloured, and with the fins down it is well-camouflaged. The fins are ornamented with blue and black. The ventral fin has a separate spine and several strong rays that are separate from the rest, looking somewhat like fingers, hence the common name. The spinous section of the dorsal fin has elongated spines with broad membranes, and juveniles have a large eye-like spot low on the membrane. When feeding it looks for small crustaceans on the bottom and glides along in a hopping fashion. When disturbed it erects its fins, showing a bright blue colour to startle intruders. They live in sand and mudflats and slopes, often in just a few metres' depth, and bury themselves in the sand when resting. This species is widespread in the tropical Indo-Pacific, ranging into subtropical zones.

Juvenile

119

Crab-eyed Goby *Signigobius biocellatus* TL 10cm

This interesting little fish has two eye-like spots in the dorsal fins and when approached these are raised and the fish moves its black lower fins in and out, looking like a crab walking sideways. Adults are usually seen in pairs, and shelter and nest in a burrow made under a solid object on sand. These gobies feed on small invertebrates filtered from the sand or mud through the gills. They prefer still, sandy, often silty areas along the bases of reefs and have a small home range. The species occurs throughout the tropical west Pacific and is only common in its specific habitat.

Golden-head Sleeper Goby *Valenciennea strigata* TL 14cm

Sleeper gobies are nearly always in pairs. The bright orange or golden head with an iridescent blue stripe over the cheek easily identifies this species. They typically hover just above the bottom, usually sand from which they filter food. Pairs usually take turns at this while the

partner keeps watch. They build a number of nesting sites in their area out of dead coral, sticks or whatever they can find. On dusk the holes are closed over and usually the male takes care of the last one and dives through the 'invisible door'. This is a common species which is widespread in the tropical Indo-Pacific.

Red-lined Goby *Amblygobius rainfordi* TL 85mm

These slow swimmers usually hover almost motionless between coral walls or on the sides of large coral bases. A distinctive species with a series of red longitudinal stripes, outlined with blue, and white spots along the base of the second dorsal fin. The snout is often yellow and the colour gradually changes to grey on the body, darkening towards the tail. Juveniles are virtually identical to adults. Usually they are common locally and seen in small numbers spread out on small sections in clearwater lagoons and on coastal reef slopes with rich coral growth. Widespread in the tropical west Pacific.

Black-chest Shrimp Goby *Amblyeleotris guttata* TL 11cm

These gobies live together with pale big-nipper shrimps which dig their burrows while the goby stands guard. A pale-coloured species with orange spots over most of the body, and a black ventral fin with the black extending on to the body, in front and on to the belly. Feeds on plankton drifting past and small invertebrates filtered from mouthfuls of sand taken from the bottom. Adults occur nearly always in pairs, and usually two shrimps share their burrow. Mainly found on coastal reefs and in protected inner reef lagoons in rubble zones along the bases of reefs. A widespread species in the tropical Indo-Pacific.

121

Twin-spotted Shrimp Goby *Vanderhorstia ambanoro* TL 12cm

This species lives with yellowish or brown big-nipper shrimps that dig their burrows. The body is mostly pale grey and usually has a series of double spots over the back; sometimes these spots join and form short vertical bars. Large males are ornamented with blue and pink, especially in the fins, and display to other males. They are usually

on fine or muddy bottom near solid objects where the burrow is made, and are usually seen singly. Commonly occur in sandy lagoons and coastal slopes. A widespread species in the tropical Indo-Pacific but common mainly near equatorial zones.

Red Fire Goby *Nemateleotris magnifica* TL 75mm

This small but beautiful goby is often noticed by divers as it hovers in pairs close to their burrow. The white body and red tail, combined with the tall white spine in the dorsal fin, is unmistakable. They regularly flick this spine, seemingly signalling each other. Red Fire Gobies feed on plankton drifting past. In Australia they are usually in clear outer reef habitat on rubble bottom in depths of 20m or more, but somewhat shallower in New South Wales. This photograph was taken off Coffs Harbour in 15m depth. The Red Fire Goby ranges throughout the tropical west Pacific and is common in Indonesia.

Lined Surgeonfish *Acanthurus lineatus* TL 35cm

The tail spine that is used for defence is venomous. Species is easily identified by the bright yellow or orange and blue stripes over the body. Juveniles are similar to adults but have a less lunate tail fin. Usually adults occur on shallow outer reef crests in gutters and channels where they school. Juveniles settle among rocky boulders in shallow protected areas and stay close to the bottom, quickly hiding if approached. They feed mainly on algaes scraped from flat rock or dead coral surfaces. A widespread species throughout the tropical Indo-Pacific, and young expatriate to subtropical zones with warm currents.

Blue Tang *Paracanthurus hepatus* TL 20–30cm

This species is also known as the 'number-six' fish, amongst other names, because of its black side marking shaped like the number nine or six. This mark, the brilliant blue sides and the yellow tail make identification easy. Small juve-

niles form schools on coral plates with close-set branches and feed just above on zooplankton. Quickly dive into the corals at the slightest disturbance. Adults are more daring and swim in small groups high above the bottom to feed, or wander over the bottom to graze on algae from rocks or dead corals. A widespread species in the tropical Indo-Pacific.

Moorish Idol *Zanclus cornutus* TL 22cm

Adults

The Moorish Idol is similar to the bannerfish with its long white extended spine in the dorsal fin but has a long protruding snout. Closely related to surgeonfishes, but lack the spines or plates on the tail that are characteristic of surgeonfishes. Adult Moorish Idols develop a sturdy spine in front of the eyes. The distinctive shape easily identifies this fish and it is commonly noticed by divers and snorkellers. It occurs on coastal and offshore reefs to depths of about 25m where it feeds by scraping algae off rocks or dead corals. It is widespread in the tropical Indo-Pacific and ranges into subtropical zones with larvae carried far from the spawning areas.

Juveniles

Lined Rabbitfish *Siganus lineatus* TL 40cm

Rabbitfishes have seven spines in the anal fin instead of one to three as in most other reef fishes. They are also unusual in having a spine at each end of the ventral fin with three rays in-between. All fin spines are venomous, and a stab from these is extremely painful. Many species live in seagrass habitats and are dull coloured and difficult to identify. The reef dwellers have distinctive colouration. Often seen hovering in small groups near caves, feeding on plankton, and occasionally on the move feeding on benthic algae. One of the most common species on Australian reefs, ranging to eastern New Guinea.

Foxface *Siganus vulpinus* TL 25cm

A very distinctive rabbit-fish with a bright yellow body, and a black-and-white face. The snout is longer than in other rab-bitfishes, and adults usu-ally swim in pairs. Small juveniles are secretive in densely branching corals, and often small groups are present in a large coral piece. Clear coastal

habitats to outer reef in rich coral areas, usually seen feeding between the corals and scraping algae off the bases or rocks. Common on the Great Barrier Reef. The population in northern Western Australia has a black spot on the side and is thought to be identical to the **Japanese Foxface** (*S. unimaculatus*).

Small-tooth Flounder *Pseudorhombus jenynsii* TL 35cm

This species has excellent camouflage, the ocular side matching sand or rubble perfectly. Usually four large blotches stand out from the general body pattern, spaced evenly in a square, with a fifth slightly smaller halfway to the tail. An active species during the day, and often buries itself in the sand or mud to ambush prey, but quickly dashes out when touched. They feed on benthic invertebrates and small fishes. Commonly found in sheltered bays and estuaries, and usually in silty habitats near reefs or seagrass beds. Widespread in southern waters but not known from Tasmania.

Greenback Flounder *Rhombosolea tapirina* TL 40–45cm

The ocular side of this common south coast species is sandy coloured and matches the sand on which it lays. Colour highly variable according to habitat. The snout is pointed and the body tapers towards the tail, giving this fish a diamond-shaped outline. Eyes are high and close-set. An

active species during the day, hunting shrimps and other crustaceans. Small juveniles often congregate along beaches in protected bays of large inlets and are found far up in estuaries. Adults occur in deeper parts of estuaries and bays to deep offshore on sand or mud. Restricted to Australian and New Zealand waters.

Peacock Sole *Pardachirus pavoninus* TL 22cm

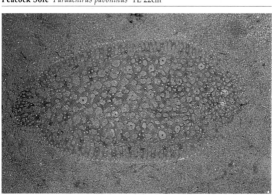

Soles are more elongated than flounders and their tail fins look like they are confluent with the dorsal and anal fins. Body colour is variable from light to dark brown, with a complicated pattern of large dark-centred pale blotches all over, bordered dark when the general colour is pale. They bury themselves during the day and hunt at night for benthic invertebrates. This fish stuns its predators with a toxin secreted from the fin ray bases along the entire body. The Peacock Sole is found on coastal sand and mud slopes, sometimes in small groups, and is a common and widespread species in the tropical Indo-Pacific.

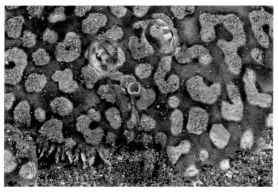

Close-up of head

127

Hawaiian Triggerfish *Rhinecanthus aculeatus* TL 25cm

A very distinctive triggerfish by colour and shape. The head is very large with the eye placed high and far back, while the mouth is small at the front. It has several strong canine-like teeth in the front. The body is covered with tiny plate-like scales, and the gill opening is restricted to a narrow slit. Juveniles are similar to adults. Mainly found in very shallow

habitats with rocky boulders or mixed algae and coral reef-flats in coastal bays. Juveniles settle far from the spawning ground, carried as larvae by currents. A very widespread species in the tropical Indo-Pacific.

Half-moon Triggerfish *Sufflamen chrysopterus* TL 30cm

Small juveniles are white with a yellow back, and a rounded tail fin. A black line develops between the yellow and white areas, and gradually it changes to the adult pattern, as shown in photograph. Adults swim openly on reef crests and slopes from coastal to outer reef habitats. Juveniles are mainly inshore and stay close to the bottom and their hiding places, usually small holes in dead reef or under rocks. Often juveniles are common and in small loose groups, spread out along small boulder zones where reef runs on to sand. This is a widespread triggerfish in the tropical Indo-Pacific, and juveniles commonly range into subtropical zones.

Clown Triggerfish *Balistoides conspicillum* TL 35cm

Adults

This is the best known triggerfish with an unmistakable colour pattern that is dominated by large round white spots on a black background. Adults are seen nearly always singly and usually swimming along steep walls on outer reefs adjacent to deep water, and holed up in caves or ledges. Small juveniles are secretive and live in caves in deep water, but some are found in New South Wales on rocky reefs in only 10m depth. A sought-after aquarium fish, but it can be very aggressive towards other fish and the strong teeth can do a lot of damage. It is widespread in the tropical Indo-Pacific, and juveniles range into subtropical zones.

Juvenile

Six-spine Leatherjacket *Meuschenia freycineti* TL 50cm

Great differences between the sexes. Males with blue and yellow but highly variable and with local forms. New South Wales males have a large yellow blotch on their sides that is mostly absent on south coast populations. Males have a set of six small spines on each side of the tail. Females are dull

brown or green and have several broad longitudinal brown bands. Small juveniles are bright green and live in weeds and seagrasses. Adults also mainly on deep reefs with sponges. A common leatherjacket in coastal waters, entering shallow bays and estuaries. A widespread temperate Australian species.

Toothbrush Leatherjacket *Acanthaluteres vittiger* TL 32cm

Great differences between the sexes and juveniles. Males are multicoloured with a patch of bristles near the tail. Females are rather plain greenish or brownish over the upper part of the body, with a blotched pattern or pale spotting and yellowish white below. Juveniles are usually bright green with a white streak on their sides, and live secretively in seagrasses. Adults are found on seagrasses and algae and sponge reefs, often swimming in large schools of mainly females high above the reef. Large adults are sometimes found in pairs as shown in photograph. This is a common species on shallow coastal reefs and ranging to deep offshore reefs. Known only in Australian waters.

Fan-belly Leatherjacket *Monacanthus chinensis* TL 40cm

A deep-bodied leatherjacket, adults characterised by the large movable skin flap below their belly. In juveniles this is not developed. Colour is drab brown to grey with indistinct banding or mottled pattern. Species best recognised by the strongly concave dorsal profile of the snout. Lives deep in the tropical zones on muddy substrates. It ranges north from Australia to Java and China seas to southern Japan, a distribution pattern characteristic of a number of other reef fishes. Although widespread in tropical waters, it is only commonly seen in coastal New South Wales waters and at similar latitudes in Western Australia.

Scribbled Leatherjacket *Aluterus scriptus* TL 1m, usually less

One of the most widespread leatherjackets or filefishes in tropical oceans. Yellow or dull brown to grey, often with iridescent blue spots or scribbles all over. Adults develop an extremely long tail. Juveniles often have a prolonged pelagic stage, drifting with floating weeds in open oceans and consequently travel great distances. When juveniles reach shore, they settle on muddy slopes and are often found on isolated pieces of junk on open bottom, or float along vertically with the head down, looking like a leaf. Adults usually solitary on deeper coastal reefs or in lagoons. Common in tropical waters, rare in southern waters.

Long-nose Filefish *Oxymonacanthus longirostris* TL 10cm

A small, brightly coloured species of tropical leatherjacket, easily identified by colour and shape. Slender body is green with orange spots; long tubed snout with small mouth at the tip. Almost exclusively lives with dense branching hard-corals, feeding on the polyps that are an important ingredient of their diet. Juveniles swim in small groups, but adults usually in pairs. Unlike other filefishes or leatherjackets that have pelagic eggs, this species has nests at the base of corals and guards the eggs like the closely related triggerfishes. Mainly found on clear coastal to outer reef crests and is widespread in the tropical Indo-Pacific.

Pygmy Leatherjacket *Brachaluteres jacksonianus* TL 9cm

With its distinctive rounded, deep body shape, this species is able to inflate its abdomen like a pufferfish. Variable in colour from brown to green and often with small white-edged dark spots all over. Males territorial and often fight by biting each other on the mouth. Display by extending their large flap under the head that reaches to the anus (*see* photograph). They feed on various invertebrates and some algae. Adults usually form pairs, juveniles solitary in weeds. At night it anchors itself by biting on to weeds. Often abundant on shallow coastal reefs in weedy or algae-covered rocks. A temperate species restricted to Australian waters.

132

Ornate Cowfish *Aracana ornata* TL 15cm

Temperate boxfishes with spines above the eyes are usually called cowfishes. The male Ornate Cowfish is ornamented with blue and orange, especially the tail which has iridescent blue loops on an orange background. The female has an intriguing pattern of stripes over the body with rings over the top, and a series of large spines along the body ridges which are reduced in males to above the eyes. Tiny juveniles are almost black. Mainly occur in very shallow habitats of mixed seagrass and low reef on sand where they feed on the bottom, on worms and other soft-bodied invertebrates. Common in the Bass Strait region.

Thorny-back Cowfish *Lactoria fornasini* TL 20cm

This species of tropical boxfish is grey to yellow, often with numerous blue scribbles all over. It has a distinctive large spine in the middle of the back. There is little difference between various stages or between the sexes. It lives singly on open bottom along reef margins where sparse algae growth or soft corals and sponges are present. Often found sheltering inside sponges. Feeds on various invertebrates on the bottom that are exposed by blowing sand with its mouth. It is widespread in the tropical Indo-Pacific, ranging into subtropical zones as an adult.

Black Boxfish *Ostracion meleagris* TL 15–20cm

Male

There are great differences between the sexes. The juvenile to female stages are jet-black with numerous tiny white spots all over. Males keep this pattern over the back, but the sides turn blue and have orange spots. This is a common but secretive species and usually only the males are observed. Females are normally nearby but probably hiding in the reef in small caves or amongst boulders and very difficult to see in the shade because of their dark colouration. This species inhabits seaward reefs in clearwater lagoons and reef crests with lots of crevices and holes to swim through. Feeds on rubble patches between corals on benthic invertebrates. It is broadly distributed in the tropical Indo-Pacific and juveniles range into sub-tropical zones.

Female

Starry Toadfish *Arothron stellatus* TL 1.2m

The Starry Toadfish is one of the largest and bulkiest pufferfishes. The colour pattern changes from lines when young to spotted as an adult. A striped pattern often remains on the belly until reaches a large size. Tiny juveniles settle in muddy coastal areas, often far from reefs. Often larger juveniles are found sleeping during the day in small depressions in the sand or mud and may partly bury themselves. Large adults live on coastal reef slopes adjacent to deep water and are seen mostly at night when they are active. A common species widely distributed in the tropical Indo-Pacific.

Black-spotted Pufferfish *Arothron nigropunctatus* TL 30cm

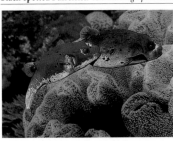

Males of this solitary species bite females with which they want to spawn (*see* photograph). Highly variable in colour, mostly grey with black spots sparsely scattered over the body but sometimes the spots are missing or more numerous. Males are usually

bright yellow or orange underneath, and sometimes the entire fish is yellow with just black around the mouth. They feed on a variety of invertebrates but often target worms in the sand. Commonly found on reef crests in coastal waters with rich invertebrate growth. A widespread species in the tropical Indo-Pacific.

Ringed Toadfish *Omegophora armilla* TL 25cm

This temperate pufferfish looks like its stocky tropical cousin. It is best identified by the large black circle around the pectoral-fin base. A second very similar species, the **Blue-spotted Toadfish** (*O. cyanopunctatus*), lacks the black ring and has numerous iridescent blue spots all over. This species is known only from south-western reefs. The Ringed Toadfish occurs primarily on deep reefs and usually hangs around caves, but is occasionally found in deeper parts of bays and under jetties in depths of 10m or more. It is a solitary species that feeds on benthic invertebrates and worms during the day. Restricted to Australian waters.

Smooth Toadfish *Tetractenos glaber* TL 15cm

Small pufferfish best identified by the spots on the back, some of which form bands, and the reddish-coloured tail and dorsal fins. Feeds on almost anything, from bottom invertebrates to plankton, and is active day and night. Sleeps by burying itself in the sand with just the eyes exposed. Commonly caught on lines around jetties and considered a nuisance fish and is usually killed. Sometimes left drying on the shores, but the poison remains for a long time and has the potential to kill a cat. Forms schools in protected coastal bays and along reef margins and enters estuaries, sometimes swimming up freshwater streams.

Clown Toby *Canthigaster callisterna* TL 25cm, usually much smaller

A subtropical member of a small group of mainly tropical sharp-nosed pufferfishes. Easily recognised by the distinctive colouration and parallel stripes along the body. Lives on clear coastal reefs and on the base of deep rock walls swimming on rubble bottom. Small juveniles secretive in ledges with sea-urchins; adults often in pairs, swimming about openly and often high in the water column. They feed on a variety of invertebrates and worms, taken from rock surfaces and rubble on sand. This species grows much larger than the tropical cousins. Restricted to Australian and New Zealand waters and common in southern New South Wales.

Saddled Puffer *Canthigaster valentini* TL 10cm

This is the most common small tropical pufferfish, often noticed because of the distinctive black saddles. They swim about openly on shallow reefs, sometimes in pairs, and are left alone by most predators as they are poisonous to eat. The **Mimic Filefish** (*Paraluteres prionurus*) is a perfect copy, and only close examination may reveal the extra dorsal fin. Small Saddled Puffer juveniles are

secretive in ledges, often with sea-urchins. Adults are territorial and males often fight, biting each other on the mouth. They feed on small invertebrates and worms from sponges and rock surfaces. It is widespread in the tropical Indo-Pacific.

137

Globe Fish *Diodon nichthemerus* TL 28cm

As a member of the porcupinefish family, this temperate species has long yellow spines and lacks the small black spots on the body that are commonly found in other species. It is active at night, moving over open bottom to feed mainly on benthic invertebrates, and hides in reef or weed during

the day, but often hovers in schools under jetties. The Globe Fish occurs in various habitats, from shallow estuaries to deep offshore and in still as well as surge zones. It is common on Australia's southern coast but is found north to Seal Rocks in New South Wales.

Blotched Porcupinefish *Diodon liturosus* TL 45cm

This is a distinctive species with large black blotches bordered with white. Usually seen at night when most active, swimming over open bottom in search of food. Diet of adults comprises mainly benthic invertebrates. During the day, it hides in caves or below shelf-type corals. Small juveniles are pelagic and drift on the surface

with weeds. They often float into shallow lagoons where they settle, hiding under large coral pieces during the day until they reach a certain size and move to deeper water. Occurs mainly in clear coastal to outer reef habitats, usually on slopes adjacent to deep water. Broadly distributed in the tropical Indo-Pacific.

Three-bar Porcupinefish *Dicotylichthys punctulatus* TL 43cm

Adult

This species has short spines and fine black spotting all over the body and usually three black bars evenly spaced from below the eye to mid-body. Diet comprises various invertebrates, but large adults often float mid-water near reef and feed on jellyfish. The Three-bar Porcupine-fish occurs on coastal to outer reef habitats, and juveniles enter estuaries. A subtropical species that variably ranges south to north-eastern Tasmania but is killed off with cold currents. The normal range is rarely south of the New South Wales border, and even in southern New South Wales there is the occasional kill with many dead individuals washing up on beaches.

Juvenile

Glossary

Abdomen. Belly, contains digestive and reproductive organs.

Adipose. Fatty.

Aggregations. Form of schooling, usually small groups of individuals gathering together.

Anal. Behind the anus.

Ascidian. Seasquirt.

Axil. Angular region on the body at the base of the pectoral fin.

Barbel. Fleshy tentacle-like extension, usually near the mouth.

Benthic. Living close to or on the bottom.

Bryozoa. Group of tiny colonial animals, forming various structures that are often coral- or plant-like.

Canine. Long conical tooth.

Carapace. Hard outer shell covering the body.

Caudal. Of or pertaining to the tail.

Cephalopod. Class of molluscs, including cuttlefish, octopus and squid.

Clasper. Male organs to transmit sperm (sharks and rays).

Compressed. Flattened laterally, from sides.

Ctenoid. Scales with spiny edges or surface.

Cycloid. Scales, generally with smooth edges or surface.

Demersal. Found on or near the bottom.

Dentition. Number, kind and combination of teeth.

Depressed. Flattened dorsally, from above.

Disc. Body shape, combined with head and pectoral fins, of greatly flattened stingrays and skates.

Dorsal. Pertaining to the back.

Expatriate. A species that occurs outside its breeding range, often juveniles carried by currents during the larval stage.

Finlet. Small fin-like structures, usually in series in tuna, following dorsal fins.

Gill opening. Exhaust for water flow through gills.

Gills. Lung function or respiration chambers.

Intertidal. Zone that covers the area between high and low tide marks.

Keel. Reinforced ridge on body, often on caudal peduncle or head.

Lanceolate. Spear-shaped or broadly pointed, often refers to caudal fin.

Larva. Immature stage, usually differing greatly from adult.

Lateral. Pertaining to the sides.

Lateral line. Sensory canal system, ranging from simple tubes to complicated pressure cells in a series along the sides, often penetrating through scales in tubes or cut-outs (notched).

Lunate. Shaped like a crescent moon (usually refers to caudal fin).

Mimicry. The act of an organism purposely resembling another.

Mysid. Small, shrimp-like crustacean.

Nape. Upper part of the head over and behind the eyes.

Nictitating membrane. Thin membrane which can be drawn across eye for protection.

Nocturnal. Active at night.

Opercle. Upper bony edge of the gill cover.

Paired fins. Pectoral and ventral fins, usually on sides, immediately following gill openings.

Pectoral fins. Uppermost of the paired fins, usually on the sides immediately behind the gill openings.

Peduncle. Body part from end of anal fin to caudal-fin base.

Pelagic. Oceanic, belonging to the open sea.

Plankton. Organisms drifting freely in the water column.

Plate. Modified hardened scale usually in tile-like arrangement, forming skin in boxfishes, pipefishes and seahorses.

Posterior. Towards the rear or tail.

Postlarva. Larva after the absorption of the yolk.

Precaudal pit. Small indentation in tail, just in from edge of fin, in sharks.

Preopercle. Front part of the operculum, an angled bone below and behind the eye.

Protrusible. Greatly expandable (usually referring to jaw).

Ring. Modified hardened scale in the shape of a ring, usually around the tail of pipefishes and seahorses.

Spiracle. Opening behind the eye, leading to gill and mouth cavity, occurs in most sharks and rays.

Striation. Narrow stripe, streak or ridge.

Substrate. The bottom.

Subterminal. Situated near but not at the end of something.

Thorn. Short, broad-based spine.

Truncate. A mainly straight vertical posterior edge of the caudal fin.

Tubercle. Short, blunt spine.

Ventral. Of or pertaining to the underside.

Ventral fins. The lower-most paired fins along the underside.

Zooplankton. Small animals (usually microscopic) drifting freely in the water column.

Further reading

Allen, G.R. and Swainston, R. (1988). *The Marine Fishes of North-Western Australia.* Western Australian Museum, Perth.

Gomon, M.F., Glover, C.J.M. and Kuiter, R.H. (1994). *The Fishes of Australia's South Coast.* State Print, Adelaide.

Hutchins, J.B. and Swainston, R. (1986). *Sea Fishes of Southern Australia.* Western Australian Museum, Perth.

Hutchins, J.B. and Thompson, M. (1983). *The Marine and Estuarine Fishes of South-Western Australia.* Western Australian Museum, Perth.

Kuiter, R.H. (1993). *Coastal Fishes of South-Eastern Australia.* Crawford House Press, Bathurst.

Kuiter, R.H. (1996). *Guide to Sea Fishes of Australia.* New Holland Publishers, Sydney.

Last, P.R. and Stevens, J. (1994). *Sharks and Rays of Australia.* CSIRO Press, Melbourne.

Last, P.R., Scott, E.O.G. and Talbot, F.H. (1983). *Fishes of Tasmania.* Tasmanian Fisheries Development Authority, Hobart.

Randall, J.E., Allen, G.R. and Steene, R.C. (1990). *Fishes of the Great Barrier Reef and Coral Sea.* Crawford House Press, Bathurst.

Index

Abudefduf sexfasciatus, 99
Acanthaluteres vittiger, 130
Acanthistius ocellatus, 52
  A. serratus, 52
Acanthopagrus australis, 72
Acanthurus lineatus, 123
Achoerodus viridis, 103
Aetapcus maculatus, 49
Aetobatus narinari, 19
Alabes dorsalis, 31
Alfonsinos, 38
Aluterus scriptus, 131
Amblyeleotris guttata, 121
Amblygobius rainfordi, 121
Amphiprion akindynos, 102
Anampses neoguinaicus, 107
Anemonefish, Barrier Reef, 102
  Spine-cheek, 102
Angelfish, Blue and Gold, 90
  Emperor, 89
  Half-circled, 89
  Keyhole, 91
  Regal, 91
  Scribbled, 90
Angelshark, 13
Anglerfish, Clown, 29
  Sargassum, 27
  Smooth, 28
  Striped, 29
  Tasselled, 28
Antennarius maculatus, 29
  A. striatus, 29
Aplodactylus arctidens, 96
Apogon cyanosoma, 64
  A. limenus, 65
  A. properuptus, 64
  A. victoriae, 65
Aptychotrema vincentiana, 15
Aracana ornata, 133
Arothron nigropunctatus, 135
  A. stellatus, 135
Aspasmogaster tasmaniensis, 30
Aspidontus taeniatus, 110
Atypichthys strigatus, 82
Aulopus purpurissatus, 25
Aulostomus chinensis, 40

Balistoides conspicillum, 129
Bannerfish, Reef, 88
  Schooling, 88
Basslet, Fairy, 57
  Mirror, 57
  Orange, 56
  Red, 56
Batfish, Tall-fin, 92
Beardy, Largetooth, 32
Big-eye Jack, *see* Trevally, Big-eye
Bigeye, Crescent-tail, 63
Blackfish, 80

Blenny, 110
  Red-streaked, 115
  Tube-worm, 117
  Two-colour Combtooth, 116
  Yellow-lined Harptail, 116
Boarfish, Long-snout, 93
Bodianus axillaris, 103
Bovichtus angustifrons, 115
Boxfish, Black, 134
Brachaluteres jacksonianus, 132
Brachionichthys hirsutus, 27
Bream, 72
  Monocle, 70
  Silver, 72
  Yellow-finned, 72
Bullseye, Common, 78
Butterflyfish, Blue-dash, 86
  Chevroned, 87
  Dusky, 85
  Goldbanded, 83
  Gunther's, 86
  Long-nose, 87
  Rainford's, 83
  Saddled, 84
  Threadfin, 84
  Vagabond, 85

Caesio caerulaurea, 76
  C. cuning, 76
Caesioperca rasor, 58
Cale, Rainbow, 111
Callorhinchus milii, 20
Canthigaster callisterna, 137
  C. valentini, 137
Caranx sexfasciatus, 68
Carcharhinus melanopterus, 14
Cardinalfish, Orange-lined, 64
  Southern Orange-lined, 64
  Sydney, 65
  Tiger, 64
  Western Striped, 65
Catfish, Coral, 24
  Striped, 24
Centroberyx gerrardi, 38
Centropogon australis, 45
  C. latifrons, 45
  C. marmoratus, 45
Centropyge bicolor, 90
  C. tibicen, 91
Cephalopholis miniata, 53
Cetoscarus bicolor, 112
Chaetodon aureofasciatus, 83
  C. auriga, 84
  C. ephippium, 84
  C. flavirostris, 85
  C. guentheri, 86
  C. plebeius, 86
  C. rainfordi, 83
  C. trifascialis, 87
  C. vagabundus, 85

Chaetodontoplus duboulayi, 90
Cheilinus fasciatus, 104
Cheilio inermis, 110
Cheilodactylus nigripes, 95
Cheilodipterus macrodon, 64
Chelmon rostratus, 83
Choerodon fasciatus, 104
Chromis hypsilepis, 100
Chrysophrys aurata, 72
Cirrhitichthys falco, 96
Cirripectes stigmaticus, 115
Clingfish, Long-snout, 30
  Tasmanian, 30
  Western Cleaner, 31
Cochleoceps bicolor, 31
Cod, Deepsea, 32
  Footballer, 53
  Long-finned, 54
  Red, 32
  see also Rockcod
Coralfish, Beaked, 83
Coris gaimard, 109
  C. picta, 108
Cowfish, Ornate, 133
  Thorny-back, 133
Cristiceps aurantiacus, 118

Dactylopus dactylopus, 119
Damsel, Blue, 100
  Immaculate, 98
  Royal, 99
Dascyllus aruanus, 101
  D. melanurus, 101
Dendrochirus zebra, 48
Devil, Eastern Blue, 61
  Southern Blue, 60
Diademichthys lineatus, 30
Diagramma labiosum, 73
Dicotylichthys punctulatus, 139
Diodon liturosus, 138
  D. nichthemerus, 138
Diploprion bifasciatum, 58
Dottyback, Multicolour, 59
  Two-tone, 59
Dragonet, Fingered, 119
Drummer, Brassy, 79
  Silver, 79
  Snubnose, 79

Ecsenius bicolor, 116
Eel, Banded Snake, 21
  Ribbon, 21
  Shore, 31
Elagatis bipinnulata, 67
Elephant Fish, 20
Emperor, Big-eye, 70
  Gold-spot, 71
  Long-snouted, 71
  Red, 74
  Small-tooth, 71
  Yellow, 58
Enoplosus armatus, 94
Epinephelus fasciatus, 55
  E. quoyanus, 54
Eucrossorhinus dasypogon, 12

Filefish, Long-nose, 132
   Mimic, 137
Filicampus tigris, 44
Flathead, Dusky, 51
   Sand, 51
Flounder, Greenback, 126
   Small-tooth, 126
Forcipiger flavissimus, 87
Fortesque, 45
   Northern, 45
   Western, 45
Foxface, 125
   Japanese, 125
Fusilier, Gold-band, 76
   Robust, 76
   Southern, 76

Garfish, Southern, 33
Ghostpipefish, Ornate, 41
Girella tricuspidata, 80
   G. zebra, 80
Glaucosoma hebraicum,
   62
Globe Fish, 138
Gnathodentex
   aurolineatus, 71
Goatfish, Black-spot, 77
   Yellow-saddle, 77
Gobbleguts, Eastern, 65
   Southern, 65
Goby, Black-chest Shrimp,
   121
   Crab-eyed, 120
   Golden-head Sleeper,
   120
   Red Fire, 122
   Red-lined, 121
   Twin-spotted Shrimp,
   122
Groper, Eastern Blue, 103
Grubfish, Lyre-tail, 114
   Spotted, 114
Gurnard, Eastern Spiny,
   50
   Southern Spiny, 50
Gymnothorax favagineus,
   22
   G. prasinus, 23
   G. undulatus, 22

Haletta semifasciata, 111
Halichoeres hortulanus,
   106
Handfish, Spotted, 27
Harlequin Fish, 52
Hawkfish, Coral, 96
   Longnose, 97
   Ring-eyed, 97
Heniochus acuminatus,
   88
   H. diphreutes, 88
Heteroclinus johnstoni,
   118
Heterodontus galeatus,
   10
   H. portusjacksoni, 10
   H. zebra, 10
Hippocampus breviceps,
   42
   H. whitei, 42
Histrio histrio, 27
Hogfish, Coral, 103
Hoplostethus atlanticus,
   35

Hulafish, Eastern, 60
   Noarlungae, 60
   Southern, 60
Humbug, 101
   Black-tail, 101
Hypnos monopterygium, 16
Hypoplectrodes annulatus,
   55
   H. maccullochi, 55
   H. nigroruber, 55
Hyporhamphus australis,
   33
   H. melanochir, 33

Indianfish, Red, 49

Jewfish, West Australian,
   62
John Dory, 39

Kingfish, Yellow-tail, 66
Kyphosus cinerascens, 79
   K. sydneyanus, 79
   K. vaigiensis, 79

Labroides dimidiatus, 110
Lactoria fornasini, 133
Latridopsis forsteri, 95
Latris lineata, 95
Leatherjacket, Fan-belly,
   131
   Pygmy, 132
   Scribbled, 131
   Six-spine, 130
   Toothbrush, 130
Lepidotrigla papilio, 50
   L. pleuracanthica, 50
Lethrinus microdon, 71
Lionfish, Common, 48
   Soldier, 48
   Zebra, 48
Lizardfish, Painted, 25
   Variegated, 26
Longtom, Crocodile, 34
Lotella rhacina, 32
Luderick, 80
Lutjanus carponotatus, 74
   L. kasmira, 75
   L. quinquelineatus, 75
   L. sebae, 74

Mackerel, Jack, 67
Macropharyngodon choati,
   106
Mado, 82
Maori, Banded, 104
Mecaenichthys
   immaculatus, 98
Meiacanthus lineatus, 116
Mendosoma lineatum, 95
Meuschenia freycineti, 130
Microcanthus strigatus, 81
Monacanthus chinensis,
   131
Monkfish, 13
Monotaxis grandoculis, 70
Moonlighter, 82
Moorish Idol, 88, 124
Moray, Green, 23
   Honeycomb, 22
   Undulate, 22
   White-eyed, 23
Myrichthys colubrinus, 21
Myripristis murdjan, 37

Nannygai, 38
Narcine tasmaniensis, 16
Neatypus obliquus, 81
Nemateleotris magnifica,
   122
Neoglyphidodon melas, 99
Neoniphon sammara, 37
Neopataecus waterhousii,
   49
Neosebastes
   scorpaenoides, 45
Nesogobius spp., 28
Notolabrus gymnogenis,
   105
Numbfish, 16
   Tasmanian, 16

Odax acroptilus, 111
Ogilbyina
   novaehollandiae, 59
Old Wife, 94
Omegophora armilla, 136
   O. cyanopunctata, 136
Ophthalmolepis lineolata,
   108
Orectolobus maculatus, 12
   O. ornatus 12
Ostracion meleagris, 134
Othos dentex, 52
Oxycirrhites typus, 97
Oxymonacanthus
   longirostris, 132

Paperfish, 47
Paracaesio xanthurus, 76
Paracanthurus hepatus,
   123
Paracirrhites arcatus, 97
Paraluteres prionurus,
   137
Parapercis ramsayi, 114
   P. schauinslandi, 114
Paraplesiops bleekeri, 60
   P. meleagris, 60
Pardachirus pavoninus,
   127
Parequula melbournensis,
   69
Parma victoriae, 98
Parrotfish, Surf, 112
   Two-colour, 112
   Yellow-head, 113
Parupeneus cyclostomus,
   77
   P. signatus, 77
Pataecus fronto, 49
Pelatus octolineatus, 62
Pempheris multiradiata,
   78
Pentaceropsis
   recurvirostris, 93
Perch, Barber, 58
   Magpie, 95
   Ruddy Gurnard, 45
Phycodurus eques, 43
Phyllophryne scortea, 28
Phyllopteryx taeniolatus,
   43
Pictilabrus laticlavius, 105
Pipefish, Tiger, 44
Plagiotremus
   rhinorynchos, 117
Platax teira, 92

143

Platycephalus bassensis, 51
P. fuscus, 51
Plectorhinchus lineatus, 73
Plectropomus laevis, 53
    P. leopardus, 54
    P. maculatus, 54
Plotosus lineatus, 24
Pomacanthus imperator,
    89
    P. semicirculatus, 89
Pomacentrus coelestis, 100
Pomatomus saltatrix, 66
Porcupinefish, Blotched,
    138
    Three-bar, 139
Premnas biaculeatus, 102
Priacanthus hamrur, 63
Prowfish, Warty, 49
    Whiskered, 49
Pseudanthias cooperi, 56
    P. dispar, 57
    P. pleurotaenia, 57
    P. squamipinnis, 56
Pseudocaranx dentex, 68
    P. wrighti, 68
Pseudochromis
    paccagnellae, 59
Pseudorhombus jenynsii,
    126
Pterois miles, 48
    P. volitans, 48
Pufferfish, Black-spotted,
    135
    Saddled, 137
Puller, One-spot, 100
Pygoplites diacanthus, 91

Rabbitfish, Lined, 125
Raja lemprieri, 17
    R. whitleyi, 17
Ray, Blue-spotted Fantail,
    19
    Eastern Fiddler, 15
    Western Shovelnose, 15
    White-spotted Eagle, 19
Rhinecanthus aculeatus,
    128
Rhinomuraena quaesita,
    21
Rhombosolea tapirina, 126
Rhycherus filamentosus,
    28
Rockcod, 32
    Bearded, 32
    Coral, 53
    Pygmy, 46
    Red, 46
    Red-barred, 55
    Southern, 46
    Western, 46
Roughy, 35
    Orange, 35
Runner, Rainbow, 67

Sargocentron rubrum, 36
    S. spiniferum, 36
Saurida nebulosa, 26
Saury, Blotched, 26
Scad, Southern Yellowtail,
    67
Scalyfin, 98
Scarus rivulatus, 112
    S. spinus, 113

Scolopsis bilineata, 70
Scorpaena cardinalis, 46
    S. papillosa, 46
    S. scaber, 46
    S. sumptuosa, 46
Scorpionfish, 47
    Leaf, 47
Scorpis lineolata, 79
Seacarp, Southern, 96
Seadragon, Leafy, 43
    Weedy, 43
Seahorse, Short-head, 42
    White's, 42
Seaperch, Banded, 55
    Black-banded, 55
    Half-banded, 55
Sergeant Baker, 25
Sergeant, Scissor-tail, 99
Seriola lalandi, 66
Shark, Blacktip Reef, 14
    Crested Horn, 10
    Port Jackson, 10
    Whitetip Reef, 14
    Zebra, 11
    Zebra Horn, 10
Siderea thyrsoidea, 23
Siganus lineatus, 125
    S. unimaculatus, 125
    S. vulpinus, 125
Signigobius biocellatus,
    120
Silver Belly, Melbourne,
    69
Skate, Melbourne, 17
    Thornyback, 17
    Whiteley's, 17
Snapper, 72
    Blue-stripe, 75
    Five-line, 75
    Red, 38
    Spanish Flag, 74
Soldierfish, Crimson, 37
Sole, Peacock, 127
Solenostomus paradoxus,
    41
Squatina australis, 13
Squirrelfish, Giant, 36
    Redcoat, 36
    Spotfin, 37
Stegastoma fasciatum, 11
Stethojulis bandanensis,
    107
Stingaree, Banded, 18
    Common, 18
    Crossback, 18
    Stripey, 81
Sufflamen chrysopterus,
    128
Surgeonfish, Lined, 123
Sweep, Footballer, 81
    Silver, 79
Sweetlips, Oblique-
    banded, 73
    Slate, 73
Synodus variegatus, 26

Taenianotus triacanthus,
    47
Taeniura lymna, 19
Tailor, 66
Tang, Blue, 123
Tetractenos glaber, 136
Thalassoma lunare, 109

Thornfish, 115
Tilodon sexfasciatus, 82
Toadfish, Blue-spotted,
    136
    Ringed, 136
    Smooth, 136
    Starry, 135
Toby, Clown, 137
Trachichthys australis, 35
Trachinocephalus myops,
    25
Trachinops
    caudimaculatus, 60
    T. noarlungae, 60
    T. taeniatus, 60
Trachurus declivisi, 67
    T. novaezelandiae, 67
Trevally, Big-eye, 68
    Skipjack, 68
    White, 68
Triaenodon obesus, 14
Triggerfish, Clown, 129
    Half-moon, 128
    Hawaiian, 128
Trout, Bar-cheek Coral, 54
    Coral, 54
    Tiger, 53
Trumpeter, Bastard, 95
    Real-bastard, 95
    Striped, 95
    Western Striped, 62
Trumpetfish, 40
Trygonoptera testacea, 18
Trygonorrhina fasciata, 15
    T. guaneria, 15
Tuskfish, Harlequin, 104
Tylosurus crocodilus, 34

Urolophus cruciatus, 18

Valenciennea strigata, 120
Vanderhorstia ambanoro,
    122
Vincentia conspersa, 65
    V. novaehollandiae, 65

Weedfish, Golden, 118
    Johnston's, 118
Whiting, Blue Weed, 111
Wirrah, Eastern, 52
    Western, 52
Wobbegong, Banded, 12
    Ornate, 12
    Spotted, 12
    Tasselled, 12
Wrasse, Black-backed, 107
    Blue-streak Cleaner, 110
    Checkerboard, 106
    Choat's, 106
    Cigar, 110
    Comb, 108
    Crimson-banded, 105
    Gaimard, 109
    Maori, 108
    Moon, 109
    Red-spot, 107
    Senator, 105

Zanclus cornutus, 88, 124
Zebra Fish, 80
Zeus faber, 39